W9-ADP-019

WITHDRAWN

The Modern Language Association of America

Selected Bibliographies in Language and Literature

Walter S. Achtert, Series Editor

1. Roger D. Lund. *Restoration and Early Eighteenth-Century English Literature, 1660–1740: A Selected Bibliography of Resource Materials*. 1980.

2. Richard Kempton. *French Literature: An Annotated Guide to Selected Bibliographies*. 1981.

3. William A. Wortman. *A Guide to Serial Bibliographies for Modern Literatures*. 1982.

A GUIDE TO SERIAL BIBLIOGRAPHIES FOR MODERN LITERATURES

William A. Wortman

LIBRARY
BRYAN COLLEGE
DAYTON, TENN. 37321

The Modern Language Association of America
New York, New York   1982

77403

Copyright © 1982 by The Modern Language Association of America

Library of Congress Cataloging in Publication Data

Wortman, William A., 1940-
   A guide to serial bibliographies for modern literatures.

   (Selected bibliographies in language and literature; 3)
   Bibliography: p.
   Includes indexes.
   1. Literature, Modern—Bibliography—Periodicals—
Bibliography.   2. Bibliography—Bibliography—
Literature, Modern.   3. Bibliography—Bibliography—
Periodicals.   I. Title.   II. Series.
Z6519.W67 [PN695]   016.805   81-18744
ISBN 0-87352-952-9   AACR2
ISBN 0-87352-953-7 (pbk.)

Published by The Modern Language Association of America
62 Fifth Avenue, New York, New York 10011

Contents

Preface

No one can begin a compilation such as this without referring to Richard Gray's *Serial Bibliographies in the Humanities and Social Sciences,* a work that not only has provided many of the titles in my list but has also been a model for its content. There are important differences, however, between Gray's work and mine. This *Guide* is more current, its audience and its range of titles are more specialized, and its coverage includes all the modern literatures. Moreover, and somewhat to my surprise, slightly over fifty percent of my titles in literature alone (not counting the subject and author bibliographies) did not appear in Gray's list. Clearly, there has been a considerable change in the bibliographic scene over the past decade. The key difference, however, is that I have tried to provide a tool for a distinct audience. This is a guide to current serial bibliographies in modern literatures of use to students of literature.

The range and depth of coverage, the arrangement of items, the intended audience, the kinds of serial bibliographies, and the exclusions and limitations are explained in the introduction. In this preface I will confine myself to apologies and thanks. Most bibliographers admit to discovering additional items, often embarrassingly significant ones, just as soon as their work is published. I expect a similar experience, the more so as I seem to have happened on an appallingly large number of entries through serendipity rather than through rigorous bibliographic searching. I hope that readers who discover omissions will let me know about them—and make appropriate notes in their own copies of this *Guide.*

Some of my indebtedness is indicated in the bibliography. I should, however, especially mention my gratitude for the fine collections of the Columbia University libraries and the New York Public Library, and for the contribution of my readers. Margaret Patterson and Vincent Tollers read two drafts of this work and made many sensible suggestions about style and format, and, more important, they corrected errors of detail and called my attention to additional bibliographies. Without their diligence this would have been a lesser work. In addition, I want to thank Donald E. Oehlerts, Director of Libraries, Miami University, who granted me timely leaves for research, the Miami University Faculty Research Committee, who provided a grant that helped defray expenses, and Sarah Barr, Miami University's Interlibrary Loan Librarian, whose help was essential to me.

Margaret Howlett and the late R. F. Howlett provided a second home for me (and showed a surprising degree of interest in an esoteric bibliography), and I would like to think of this book as an acknowledgment of their generosity.

Detailed Table of Contents

This table of contents includes the first occurrence of every numbered bibliography in Chapters i through iv but not cross-references, repeated titles, or supplementary titles. The index provides a complete list of all titles mentioned in this *Guide*.

CHAPTER FIVE. SUBJECTS

CHAPTER SIX. AUTHORS

Chapter One.   Introduction

Serial bibliographies are one of the basic tools of research and are essential at all levels. Although the most widely used are listed in the standard guides to literary study, such as Altick and Wright's *Selective Bibliography for the Study of English and American Literature*, 6th ed. (New York: Macmillan, 1979), and a complete list of them is provided in Richard Gray's *Serial Bibliographies in the Humanities and Social Sciences* (Ann Arbor: Pierian, 1969), there is no up-to-date and comprehensive list of all current serial bibliographies in all the modern literatures. It is this currentness and comprehensiveness that I have tried to achieve here. In addition, I have listed serial bibliographies in many nonliterary fields that seem to me to be important to contemporary scholars—scholars who are increasingly specialized, increasingly multidisciplinary, and increasingly varied in their interests.

Current literary scholarship is, indeed, characterized by its sheer mass, by the variety of subjects and authors studied, and by the variety of critical approaches taken. Fortunately for those who need to find and use this scholarship, there has also been an increase in the number, variety, and quality of bibliographies. The most broadly useful, the *MLA International Bibliography* (A1), is now reasonably current and its data base is accessible for computerized searches (since the 1976 volumes). At least four periodical indexes provide as close to up-to-the-minute coverage as it is possible to get (A6-A10); classification schemes and subject headings have been refined and modernized; author and specialized subject bibliographies have proliferated (see Chs. v and vi); and computers have made new types of indexing, bibliographies, and bibliographic searching possible, as exemplified most successfully (but not exclusively) in the *Arts and Humanities Citation Index* (A6). This last point deserves amplification.

Computerized typesetting and printing have made it possible to construct large bibliographic data bases. Because these data bases contain several years' worth of citations (or will in time) and because several indexing terms can be used simultaneously, it is possible to search data

1

bases faster, more thoroughly, and more precisely than it has been possible to search printed bibliographies. In addition, other new computer techniques are now available—chiefly citation, permuted title, and natural language indexing. Citation indexing, as used in the *Arts and Humanities Citation Index*, allows one to search for articles on the basis of the works cited in their text, footnotes, and bibliography. Permuted title searching, a feature of *Dissertation Abstracts International* (D128) and the *Arts and Humanities Citation Index*, allows one to search for key words in titles. Natural language indexing allows one to search a data base for any word at all, not just a predetermined list of subject terms. Thus, if it is true that literary research has been limited to those areas and subjects served by bibliographies (mainly authors, periods, and genres), then it is quite possible that literary studies will become more varied and multidisciplinary in approach and subject.

Currentness and Comprehensiveness

This *Guide* aims to include all current serial bibliographies and their direct predecessors that cover national literatures, literary periods, genres, themes and subjects, and authors. It also includes the major general and humanities indexes and bibliographies and certain selected bibliographies and indexes for subjects related to literature, to literary study, or to the literary profession. "Current" means 1975. Bibliographies being published then or later, as well as several important ones that ceased in the 1960s or early 1970s, are included. "Direct predecessors" means earlier bibliographies that developed into current ones, such as the *Bibliotheque d'Humanisme et Renaissance*, which became the *Bibliographie Internationale de l'Humanisme et de la Renaissance* (B30), and the different journals that have published the Romantic Movement bibliography (B51). Cumulations or compilations of extended runs of a bibliography are also included. The list of bibliographies in literature is intended to be exhaustive. The list of subject bibliographies, however, is selective and includes only those that are comprehensive or directly related to literary scholarship. Bibliographies for retrospective searches can be found in Gray's *Serial Bibliographies in the Humanities and Social Sciences* and such guides to literary research as Altick and Wright or Margaret Patterson's *Author Newsletters and Journals* (Detroit: Gale, 1979).

Arrangement, Cross-References, Access

The arrangement of the bibliographies here is, generally, in order from most comprehensive to most specialized. Thus, Chapter ii lists those few bibliographies that cover all literatures, as well as the general and humanities periodical indexes. Chapters iii and iv list bibliographies for individual national literatures and literary periods. Chapter v lists subject bibliographies (several of which are very comprehensive or cover large subjects). Chapter vi covers specialized author bibliographies. Frequently, however, a given topic will be covered in several different bibliographies. Someone working on William Blake, for example, should use these at least: *Blake: An Illustrated Quarterly* (E16), the eighteenth-century and Romantic Movement bibliographies (B41 and B51), the *Art Index* and *RILA* (D6 and D7), the MLA and MHRA bibliographies (A1 and B1), and the *Arts and Humanities Citation Index* (A6). It is not possible, of course, to suggest all possible bibliographies for all possible topics, but I do try throughout this *Guide* to remind readers that more comprehensive or more specialized ones exist and need to be consulted.

Within individual sections the most comprehensive or most usable bibliographies are listed first. Although I have tried to list all foreign language bibliographies, I have also generally preferred English language and North American bibliographies on the grounds that both they and the items cited in them are more likely to be available to scholars in North America.

In each section I have tried to make cross-references to those other bibliographies that are particularly relevant for the given topic and that do not have detailed subject indexing. It is important to note that a number of literary period bibliographies listed in Chapter iii are essential for research in several of the literatures included in Chapter iv. But there are a number of important indexes and bibliographies that I do not cross-reference, precisely because they do have adequate subject indexing. Among these are the general and humanities indexes (A6-A27), *Bulletin Signalétique* (A2), and *Abstracts of English Studies* (B3).

There are three ways to find items in this *Guide*: Use the detailed table of contents, which cites the first appearance of each bibliography. Follow the classified arrangement, which includes introductory and explanatory paragraphs, cross-references, and titles of predecessors and cumulations. Use the subject and title index, which cites every occurrence of every title and which allows more precise subject access than does the arrangement of Chapter v.

Audience

This *Guide* is intended for anyone studying one of the literatures included under the aegis of the Modern Language Association—undergraduates, graduate students, teaching and research faculty, librarians, scholars from other fields who need information about current literary research. These people have a wide range of interests, as any annual meeting of the MLA attests. In addition to traditional literary concerns with biography, bibliography, criticism, and literary history, there are the current concerns with new critical approaches and newly respectable authors and genres, the workaday concerns of pedagogy and professional survival, and the more or less extraliterary concerns with such matters as linguistics, libraries, and the book trade or the relations between literature and science (or art, psychology, history, or Christianity).

Kinds of Serial Bibliographies

This *Guide* is a tool with which to find predictable and readily available serial bibliographies. Other current bibliographies can be found through such indexes as the *Bibliographic Index* (D19) and the *Humanities Index* (A8). The only requirements for inclusion here, in addition to currentness, are regularity of publication and consistency of coverage. These bibliographies cover, variously, books, parts of books, festschriften and collective volumes, periodicals (mainly articles, but some notes, letters, creative writing, book reviews, and illustrations), published proceedings, audiovisual materials, dissertations and (less often) theses, unpublished papers, manuscripts, editions, translations, and reprint and microform editions. The kinds included are:

1. Comprehensive bibliographies (such as the *MLA International Bibliography* and the *Bibliographie der französischen Literaturwissenschaft*)

2. Classified bibliographies (such as the *MLA International Bibliography* and the *Bibliographie Internationale de l'Humanisme et de la Renaissance*)

3. Author bibliographies (such as those in the *James Joyce Quarterly* and the *Goethe-Jahrbuch*)

4. Subject bibliographies (such as those on the Don Juan theme and on science fiction). "Subject" refers to themes, genres, academic disciplines, and a variety of literary concerns.

5. Periodical indexes (such as the *Humanities Index* or *Periodex*)

6. Abstracting services (such as *Abstracts of English Studies* and *Philosopher's Index*)

7. Bibliographic essays (such as those in *Old English Newsletter* and *The Year's Work in Modern Language Studies*)

8. Permuted title indexes (such as in *Dissertation Abstracts International* and the *Arts and Humanities Citation Index*)

9. Citation indexes (such as the *Arts and Humanities Citation Index*)

Exclusions and Limitations

Although I have tried to include all essential serial bibliographies, there are some deliberate exclusions and limitations.

1. Trade and national bibliographies. Omitted. Besides being so numerous as to require a separate book, these are also adequately covered in Eugene Sheehy's *Guide to Reference Books*, 9th ed. (Chicago: American Library Assn., 1976, pp. 39-81; supplement, 1979, pp. 8-15).

2. Journals that regularly publish bibliographic articles on various subjects. Omitted. The coverage of such journals as *Bulletin of Bibliography* and *Modern Fiction Studies* can be found easily with regular indexes.

3. Lists of books received. Omitted. These lists can be helpful, but they are neither comprehensive nor systematic.

4. Reviews of reviews. Omitted. Formerly a common feature, these reprintings of tables of contents of related journals have been eclipsed by periodical indexes and other serial bibliographies. Exceptions: *Current Contents: Arts and Humanities* (A7) and *CALL: Current Awareness Library Literature* (D247).

5. Irregular bibliographies and bibliographic series, such as the Serif Series (Kent State Univ. Press) and the Scarecrow Press author bibliographies series. Omitted.

6. Bibliographies of current creative writing. Limited to North American writing and bibliographies. Creative writing in other countries, especially that in the non-English languages, is not covered.

7. Area studies. Limited. Geographic area studies bibliographies are included in Chapter iv, provided they list a substantial number of literary items. Subject area studies, such as black studies and women's studies, are covered in Chapter v. American studies bibliographies are listed in Chapter v.

Contents of Entries

Each entry should provide several items of information: (1) title of the bibliography or of its parent journal; (2) publisher and place of publication; (3) frequency of publication of the bibliography and its parent journal; (4) dates of publication of the bibliography and of the years covered by it (the former are noted in the entry, the latter in the annotation); (5) character of the coverage and the means of access to it (the terms used to describe these are explained below); (6) titles of direct predecessors and cumulations, if any. An asterisk after the title indicates that I have not examined the bibliography.

Terms

Most terms in the *Guide*'s annotations are self-explanatory, but some might cause confusion and so need a brief explanation.

International The bibliography covers publications from more than one country (with the U.S.A. and Canada considered as North America). In practice, "international" generally means North America, Great Britain, and Western Europe.

Comprehensive The bibliography covers many types of material, a great number of items, or a wide range of subjects. The *MLA International Bibliography* is comprehensive in all three senses; the *Stendhal Club* bibliography is narrow in its range of subjects—Stendhal—but comprehensive in the amount and kind of critical items it cites.

Classified Items in the bibliography are arranged under a variety of subject headings. The *MLA International Bibliography* is an example.

Author list Items are listed alphabetically by their authors' names.

Bibliographic essay An evaluative essay that surveys current scholarship on a subject or author.

Books Includes monographs, festschriften, and collective volumes.

Reviews Book reviews.

Articles Most indexes and bibliographies that cover periodicals confine their coverage to the major articles and omit notes, letters, illustrations, and other features. If coverage is broader than just articles, that fact is noted.

Critic index Index cites authors of scholarship, not authors of primary material.

Dates When the years covered by the bibliography are different from those of its publication, these dates of coverage are indicated in the annotation.

Chapter Two. Comprehensive Bibliographies and General Indexes

Considering the quantity and variety of current scholarship, it is not surprising that there is no single truly comprehensive bibliography for all the modern literatures. The *MLA International Bibliography* comes closest to comprehensive coverage, and it is no denigration of its achievement to point out that researchers must use other bibliographies as well if they want to find items that for one reason or another were omitted by MLA bibliographers. Although the *MLA International Bibliography* is now the single best bibliography for all the modern languages and literatures, its coverage is complemented, and in some areas surpassed, by other literature and subject bibliographies, such as the MHRA *Annual Bibliography of English Language and Literature*, the *Bibliographie der deutschen Sprach- und Literaturwissenschaft*, and the *Arts and Humanities Citation Index*. These other bibliographies can occasionally provide more up-to-date coverage, more specific or in-depth coverage, or, in the case of the major European literature bibliographies, more foreign language citations.

The *Bulletin Signalétique 523: Histoire et Science de la Littérature*, although more limited than the *MLA International Bibliography* in its coverage of materials, does deal comprehensively with literary theory and history of all literatures; in addition, it is slightly more current. The new index *LLINQUA* has coverage comparable to that of the *Bulletin Signalétique*, provides detailed subject indexing, and appears to cover studies combining linguistics and literature especially well. The *Quarterly Check-List of Literary History* was useful for the years it covered. Indexes listed in Section 2 (below), while generally emphasizing English language and English and American literature coverage, can be valuable sources for researchers in other literatures.

1. COMPREHENSIVE BIBLIOGRAPHIES

A1 *MLA International Bibliography of Books and Articles on the Modern Languages and Literatures.* New York: Modern Language Assn., 1922—. Annual.

An international, comprehensive, classified bibliography of books, articles, and dissertations, 1921—, on all modern language literatures, folklore, and linguistics. Items selected for inclusion must deal with literature; notes, letters to the editor, news, creative writing, and biographical, historical, and other articles appearing in the journals indexed are omitted. An on-line computer search capability added in 1978 covers a data base made up of all the bibliographies from 1976 on and makes it possible to search for items by words in titles, by subject terms, and by critics' names. To the virtue of comprehensiveness, then, has been added the convenience of the cumulated data base and the search power and precision of additional access points.

The bibliography was originally carried as part of *PMLA*, 1922–68; it was published in three volumes bound as one, 1969–80: Vol. I: General, English, American, Medieval and Neo-Latin, and Celtic literatures; and folklore, Vol. II: non-English language literatures, and Vol. III: linguistics. A fourth volume, 1969–72, consisted of the ACTFL bibliography (see D257).

The 1981 bibliography, published 1982, introduced a new five-volume format: Vol. I: English language literatures; Vol. II: non-English language literatures; Vol. III: linguistics; Vol. IV: general literature and related topics; and Vol. V: folklore. Each volume will have a context-preserving subject index, along with a critic index.

Breadth and depth of coverage have increased over the years, as shown in the following chart (publication dates of items cited are shown):

North American scholarship exclusively, 1921–55; international scholarship, 1956—.

Bibliographic essay format, 1921–25.

Index of critics, 1946–55, 1964—.

Linguistics listed under General Literature section and under major language groups, 1921–66; separate section, 1967—.

Folklore included under General Literature, 1926–68; separate section, 1969—. Folklore subsections continue to be a part of African, Modern Greek, and East European sections.

Number of periodicals covered; 1930—35 titles; 1940—50 titles; 1950—120 titles; 1956—775 titles; 1978—3,000 titles.

Abstracts of major articles for years 1970–75 provided in *MLA Abstracts*. 6 vols. (New York: Modern Language Association, 1972–77). Available for on-line searches, 1976—.

Coverage of the individual modern language literatures is described in Chapters iii and iv according to the scheme of the 1969–80 bibliography.

For coverage of North American scholarship prior to the MLA bibliography, see the annual reviews for 1910–19 (Vols. 1–10, 1911–20) in *The American Year Book: A Record of Events and Progress* (New York: Appleton, 1911–50). Cumulated: Arnold N. Rzepecki, *Literature and Language Bibliographies from the American Year Book, 1910–19* (Ann Arbor: Pierian, 1970).

A2   *Bulletin Signalétique 523. Histoire et Science de la Littérature.* Paris: Centre National de la Recherche Scientifique, 1948—. 4/yr.

An international, classified bibliography, for years 1947—, of articles from about 600 periodicals, reports, dissertations, congress and colloquium publications, and festschriften. Arranged by literary period. Critic and subject indexes in each issue are cumulated annually. Annotations in French.

A3   *LLINQUA: Language and Literature Index Quarterly.* Aachen, W. Germany: CoBRa, 1980—. 4/yr.

Indexes articles and book reviews in about 500 international periodicals. Critics and reviewers are listed alphabetically, followed by an author index of books reviewed and a detailed subject index (including individual authors and works).

(C63) *Beiträge zur Literaturkunde: Bibliographie ausgewählter Zeitungs- und Zeitschriftenbeiträge.*

Covers East German and German socialist publications on world literature.

(C131) *Novaia Sovetskaia Literatura po Literaturovedeniiu.*

Covers Soviet books and articles on world literature.

(C132) *Novaia Inostrannaia Literatura po Literaturovedeniiu.*

Covers non-Soviet publications on world literature.

A4 *Quarterly Check-List of Literary History: An International Index of Current Books, Monographs, Brochures, and Separates.* Darien, Conn.: American Bibliographic Service, 1958–75. 4/yr.

A checklist of books on English, American, French, and German literary history, arranged alphabetically by author.

2. PERIODICAL INDEXES

The comprehensive bibliographies listed here and in other chapters generally have two weaknesses: they are not current and they are not accessible from a variety of points. (Although the new on-line capability of the *MLA International Bibliography* does offer multiple approaches to the data base, it is expensive to use for ordinary literature searches.) There is a need for subject indexing of current periodicals and books, and five of the indexes listed here are particularly valuable: the *Arts and Humanities Citation Index*, the *Humanities Index*, the *American Humanities Index*, the *British Humanities Index*, and the *Essay and General Literature Index*. Taken together they offer currentness (within about four months of publication), subject access under a variety of headings (with each periodical article cited being listed under as many different headings as apply), coverage of some journals not covered in the MLA bibliography (especially author newsletters), thorough analytic indexing of festschriften and collective books (in the *Essay and General Literature Index*), and, in the *Arts and Humanities Citation Index*, citation and permuted title indexing.

Thorough subject indexing, such as that in the *Humanities Index*, means that one can easily find articles not only about a particular author but also about subjects like ambiguity in literature, sonnet techniques in various literatures, or science fiction. A drawback, of course, is that the subject headings or indexing terms might be insufficiently detailed or out-of-date and not indicative of current research interests. Citation indexing, now available in the *Arts and Humanities Citation Index*, has proved invaluable in science and social sciences research and should be nearly as useful for literary research because it indexes on the basis of citations (or implied—that is, unfootnoted—citations). An article on Keats with a useful aside on Joyce's *Portrait of the Artist as a Young Man*, for example, or articles based on the theoretical work of Jung, Frye, or Derrida could be found simply by searching for citations to Joyce or to the theorist. A permuted title index, another feature of the *Arts and Humanities Citation Index*, lists every key word in an article's title and so makes it possible to find articles on subjects for which there are no subject headings, if the subject term is used in the title.

Resources in Education (part of the ERIC system) is primarily concerned with pedagogical matters, but it does list some unpublished papers, especially those that have been read at national meetings or that report on significant bibliographical or research projects. By no means, however, is there an accurate and comprehensive record of unpublished papers. Published proceedings, by contrast, are adequately covered by both the *MLA International Bibliography* and the *Index to Social Sciences and Humanities Proceedings*.

Indexes to popular and general interest North American periodicals are listed in Section 3. Although their usefulness in traditional research is perhaps marginal, they can be important for research in all aspects of popular culture.

A6   *Arts and Humanities Citation Index*. Philadelphia: Inst. for Scientific Information, 1978—. 3/yr., with annual cumulation.

An author, citation, and permuted title index, for years 1976—, to articles, reviews, notes, correspondence, and creative writing and illustrations in about 1,000 international periodicals and some festschriften and collective volumes. The "Source Index" is an author list of current articles, etc.; the "Permuterm Index" is a permuted key-word-in-title index; the "Citation Index" lists all works cited in footnotes or referred to in texts of articles. Particularly useful for interdisciplinary and nontraditional studies because of its multiple access points and comprehensiveness. Supplemented by:

A7   *Current Contents: Arts and Humanities*. Philadelphia: Inst. for Scientific Information, 1978—. 52/yr.

Each weekly issue prints tables of contents of periodicals and collective volumes covered by the *Arts and Humanities Citation Index*, with critic and subject indexes. The most current of all indexes.

A8   *Humanities Index*. New York: Wilson, 1974—. 4/yr., with annual cumulation.

Comprehensive author and subject index to mainly North American scholarly journals in the humanities, history, and fine arts. Examples of subject headings are Ambiguity in Literature, Romanticism, and Sex in Literature, as well as subject authors. It is current, scans about 120 literary journals and reviews, and includes creative writing and book reviews as well as criticism. Continues, with expanded coverage, *Social Sciences and Humanities Index* (New York: Wilson, 1965–74) and *International Index to Periodicals* (New York: Wilson, 1916–65).

A9   *American Humanities Index*. Troy, N.Y.: Whitston, 1975—. 4/yr., with annual cumulation.

A comprehensive author and subject index to articles, reviews, and creative writing in North American periodicals. Coverage complements that in the *Humanities Index* and includes about 250 literary journals and author newsletters.

A10   *British Humanities Index*. London: Library Assn., 1962—. 4/yr., with annual cumulation.

A comprehensive author and subject index to British and Commonwealth journals in the humanities and fine arts (about 50 of which are literary journals). Covers criticism; book, theater, and film reviews; and creative writing. Continues the *Subject Index to Periodicals* (London: Library Assn., 1916–61).

A11   *Internationale Bibliographie der Zeitschriftenliteratur aus allen Gebieten des Wissens*. Osnabrück: Dietrich, 1965—. 12/yr.

A comprehensive author and subject index to international periodicals on all subjects. Subject headings are in German; the specificity of literary topics is not so great, however, as in the preceding four indexes. Continues the *Internationale Bibliographie der fremdsprachigen Zeitschriftenliteratur* (Leipzig: Dietrich, 1911–64).

A12   *Essay and General Literature Index*. New York: Wilson, 1934—. 2/yr., with annual cumulation.

An author and subject index, for years 1900—, to English language festschriften and collective volumes on all subjects, but with emphasis on literature and the humanities. Covers original as well as reprinted articles.

A13   *Canadian Essay and General Literature Index*. Toronto: Univ. of Toronto Press, 1975–79. Annual.

Coverage was comparable to that in the *Essay and General Literature Index* but confined to Canadian books for years 1973–75. An additional year of coverage for 1971–72 is provided by *Canadian Essays and Collections Index 1971–1972* (Ottawa: Canadian Library Assn., 1976).

A14   *Index to Social Sciences and Humanities Proceedings*. Philadelphia: Inst. for Scientific Information, 1979—. 4/yr.

An author and subject index to individual papers in published proceedings on a broad range of subjects, including literature, philology, linguistics, theater, and communication.

A15   *Resources in Education*. Washington, D.C.: National Institute of Education, 1966—. 12/yr.

Part of the ERIC system. A classified list of abstracts of documents on a variety of subjects, generally pedagogical in nature. Subject and author indexes. Includes unpublished papers read at conferences, bibliographies, and reports of research projects. Among the useful subject headings are those for annotated bibliographies, literary analysis, and individual authors. Documents are on microfiche, often available in university libraries.

3.   POPULAR AND GENERAL INTEREST INDEXES

The indexes listed here, although marginally valuable in traditional literary research, are useful for an exhaustive search of the literature or for research into popular culture. Most also lead to creative writing, as well as to book, film, and drama reviews, to some literary criticism, to biography, and to such features as interviews. Each provides author and subject indexing. Arrangement is alphabetical.

A22   *Access: The Supplementary Index to Periodicals*. Evanston, Ill.; John Gordon Burke, 1976—. 3/yr. (Syracuse, N.Y.: Gaylord, 1976–78).
A23   *Alternative Press Index: An Index to Alternative and Radical Publications*. Baltimore: Alternative Press Centre, 1969—. 4/yr.
(B84)   *Canadian Periodical Index/Index de Périodiques Canadian*.
(D392) *The Catholic Periodical and Literature Index*.
(D231) *Index to Jewish Periodicals*.
A24   *The New Periodicals Index*. Boulder, Colo.: Mediaworks, 1977—. 2/yr.

A25 *Popular Periodical Index.* Camden, N.J.: Popular Periodical Index, 1973—. 2/yr.

A26 *The Reader's Guide to Periodical Literature.* New York: Wilson, 1905—. 12/yr., with annual cumulation.

Coverage for 1880–1922 provided by *Nineteenth-Century Reader's Guide to Periodical Literature.* 2 vols. (New York: Wilson, 1944).

A27 *Vertical File Index.* New York: Wilson, 1935—. 11/yr.

A subject and title index to pamphlets on all subjects.

Chapter Three. English, American, and Commonwealth Literatures

Most of what was said in Chapters i and ii could be said again here, and the reader should consult those chapters for a discussion of serial bibliographies in general and of the coverage of this *Guide* in particular. There are at present a nearly adequate range of general bibliographies for English, American, and Commonwealth literatures and a good range of period, subject, and author bibliographies. The two major comprehensive bibliographies, the *MLA International Bibliography* (A1) and the MHRA *Annual Bibliography of English Language and Literature* (B1), display surprisingly little overlap; researchers must use both because each has features and coverage not found in the other. In addition, for more currentness and comprehensiveness and for more precise subject indexing, one must use the *Bulletin Signalétique* (A2), *LLINQUA: Language and Literature Index Quarterly* (A3), and the seven major humanities indexes (A6–A12), as well as appropriate period bibliographies in this chapter.

The bibliographies in Chapter v cover subjects ranging from American studies to women's studies and including literary genres, related academic disciplines (such as art, history, linguistics, and philosophy), comparative studies (comparative literature and the relations between literature and art, psychology, science, and religion), and literary themes and topics (such as the Don Juan theme, Arthurian studies, and American regionalism). Many English and American writers have author bibliographies included in Chapter vi.

1. GENERAL BIBLIOGRAPHIES

(A1) *MLA International Bibliography.*
   See Chapter ii for a description of coverage and features.
   B1 *Annual Bibliography of English Language and Literature.* London: Modern Humanities Research Assn., 1921—. Annual.
   An annual, international, comprehensive, and classified bibliography, for 1920—, of books, reviews, articles, and dissertations on English, American, and Commonwealth literature, English language, English folklore, bibliography, and related historical and cultural studies. Classification categories include broad subject areas (literature, language, folklore, bibliography) and subdivisions for literary periods, genres, individual authors, and various aspects of language, literature, and folklore studies. Some of these subject subdivisions are described more fully in Chapter v. American and Commonwealth writers are included

with English writers in the appropriate literary periods. Author, critic, and selective subject indexes.

Although now several years behind in its coverage, the *Annual Bibliography* must still be consulted along with the *MLA International Bibliography.*

B2 *The Year's Work in English Studies.* London: English Assn., 1921—. Annual.

Selective and evaluative bibliographic essays on the year's international books and articles dealing with English, American, and Commonwealth language and literature. Carries chapters on the literary periods, Chaucer, Shakespeare, Milton, and American literature. The essays discuss first general studies and scholarly tools and then turn to the criticism on individual authors. Author, title, and subject index (the last is especially detailed starting with 1947). Critic index.

B3 *Abstracts of English Studies.* Calgary, Alta.: Univ. of Calgary, 1958—. 4/yr. (Formerly Champaign, Ill.: National Council of Teachers of English, 1958–80.)

Publishes abstracts of articles and some monographs on general literary studies and on English, American, Commonwealth, and, to a lesser extent, world literature. The English and American sections are subdivided into literary periods (with subsections for individual authors) and four categories: particularism and regionalism, bibliography, language, and themes and types. Author, subject, and critic index in each issue.

B4 *Studies in English Literature, 1500–1900.* Houston, Texas: Rice Univ., 1961—. 4/yr.

Each issue carries a bibliographic essay on the year's international books (and an occasional article) in one of four periods: English Renaissance (winter), Elizabethan and Jacobean Drama (spring), Restoration and Eighteenth Century (summer), and Nineteenth Century (autumn).

B5 *Études Anglaises: Grande Bretagne, États-Unis.* Paris: Didier, 1937—. 4/yr.

"Theses" is a quarterly list, with summaries, of French theses (dissertations) on English and American language and literature. Coverage starts with Vol. 21, 1968.

B6 *English Studies: A Journal of English Language and Literature.* Lisse: Swets en Zeitlinger, 1919—. 6/yr.

"Current Literature," Vol. 7—, 1925—. Three bibliographic essays each year review current Commonwealth and United Kingdom creative writing, and a fourth essay reviews North American and British work in criticism, literary theory and history, and biography.

B7 *The Dutch Quarterly Review of Anglo-American Letters.* Amsterdam: Rodopi, 1971—. 4/yr.

The "Survey" section in each issue is a bibliographic essay on recent critical books and is comparable in coverage to *Studies in English Literature, 1500–1900* (B4).

B8 *English Studies in Africa: A Journal of the Humanities.* Johannesburg: Witwatersrand Univ., 1958—. 2/yr.

The "Select Bibliography" is an author list of books and articles on English language and literature by South Africans or published in South Africa (excluding those in *English Studies in Africa*).

B9 *English and American Studies in German: Summaries of Theses and Monographs. A Supplement to Anglia.* Tübingen: Niemeyer, 1969—. Annual.

An annotated list of books and dissertations from the German-speaking countries on linguistics, English and American literature, and the teaching of English. Annotated in English. Critic and subject indexes.

2. LITERARY PERIODS

Specialized period bibliographies can have several advantages over the more general listings in the MLA and MHRA bibliographies. Often, although not always, they are more up-to-date and provide a more extensive and varied list of citations. Their classification scheme or subject indexing can be more detailed and precise. They can give a more accurate picture of relevant scholarship, either through annotations and commentary or by the inclusion of studies on other subjects or other literatures. They are often, in fact, not only a record of scholarship but a guide to it.

This section is subdivided by period, and within each subsection the bibliographies are listed in order from most comprehensive to most specialized and from most to least readily available in North American libraries. Of the bibliographies and indexes already listed, only the MLA, MHRA, and *Year's Work* are repeated. The other general bibliographies should, however, be consulted, as should the humanities and general indexes in Chapter ii. The following are particularly valuable because of their subject indexing and currentness: *Arts and Humanities Citation Index* (A6), *Humanities Index* (A8), *American Humanities Index* (A9), *Essay and General Literature Index* (A12), *Abstracts of English Studies* (B3), *Bulletin Signalétique 523* (A2), and *LLINQUA: Language and Literature Index Quarterly* (A3).

Several of the author bibliographies in Chapter vi offer valuable additional citations for the relevant periods.

A. MEDIEVAL

B15 *International Medieval Bibliography.* Leeds: Univ. of Leeds, 1968—. 2/yr.

An international, comprehensive, classified bibliography, for years 1965—, of notes and articles on all aspects of medieval Europe. Categories include art, folklore, language, and literature. Critic and subject indexes in each issue.

B16 *Cahiers de Civilisation Médiévale X^e –XIIe Siècles: Bibliographie.* Poitiers: Centre d'Études Superieures de Civilisation Médiévale: 1958—. 5/yr.

Carries an annual, international bibliography of books and articles, for 1969—. Name, subject, and critic index. Appeared in each issue, Vol. 1–11, and annually in a fifth issue, Vol. 12—.

(A1) *MLA International Bibliography.*

See sections on Old English, Middle English, Medieval and Neo-Latin, and the medieval subsection under General Literature and Related Topics III. in Vol I. See the appropriate sections in Vol. II for the non-English literatures.

(B1) *Annual Bibliography of English Language and Literature.*
See the Old English and Middle English sections for general subjects and individual writers.

(B2) *The Year's Work in English Studies.*
See chapters on Old English and Middle English.

B17 *International Guide to Medieval Studies: A Continuous Index to Periodical Literature.* Darien, Conn.: American Bibliographic Service, 1962–77. 4/yr.
Provided international, comprehensive coverage of periodicals, festschriften, and published proceedings on all aspects of the medieval world. Items arranged by author, with annual author index. Detailed subject index in each issue and cumulated annually.

B18 *Quarterly Check-List of Medievalia.* Darien, Conn.: American Bibliographic Service, 1958–78. 4/yr.
A comprehensive, international list, for 1957–77, of books (studies, reprints, translations) on all aspects of the medieval world. Entries arranged alphabetically by author. Annual author, editor, and translator index.

B19 *Speculum: A Journal of Medieval Studies.* Cambridge, Mass.: Medieval Academy of America, 1926—. 4/yr.
"Bibliography of Editions and Translations in Progress of Medieval Texts," Vol. 48, 1973—, is an annual subject list of mainly North American and British projects.
A classified list of American periodical literature on medieval studies was a feature of most issues, 1934–72.

B20 *Neuphilologische Mitteilungen: Bulletin de la Société Néophilologique/Bulletin of the Modern Language Society.* Helsinki: Modern Language Soc., 1899—. 4/yr.
Publishes an annual, international list of work in progress in Old English (for 1964—), Middle English (for 1963—), and Chaucer (for 1968—). The Chaucer list is also carried in *Chaucer Review* (E40).

B21 *Old English Newsletter.* Binghamton, N.Y.: Center for Medieval and Early Renaissance Studies, 1967—. 2/yr.
"Old English Bibliography," 1969—, is an annual, international, classified bibliography of books, articles, and dissertations.
"The Year's Work in Old English Studies," 1969—, is an annual, evaluative bibliographic essay.

B22 *Anglo-Saxon England.* Cambridge: Cambridge Univ. Press, 1971—. Annual.
Carries an annual, international, comprehensive, and classified bibliography of books, significant reviews, and articles on all aspects of Anglo-Saxon culture. Sections on general, language, literature, Anglo-Latin and ecclesiastical texts, paleography, history, numismatics, archaeology, and book reviews. Places greater emphasis on history, archaeology, and Anglo-Saxon culture than does *OEN*.

B23 *Olifant: A Publication of the Société Rencesvals, American-Canadian Branch.* Winnipeg: Société Rencesvals, American-Canadian Branch, 1973—. 4/yr.
Carries a quarterly checklist of books, reviews, North American dissertations, and articles, for 1966—, on the medieval romance. Published in mimeograph format, 1966–72, by the Société.

B24 *Bulletin Bibliographique de la Société Rencesvals.* Paris: Nizet, 1958–72. Annual.

An international, classified bibliography of books, reviews, and articles on the medieval romance. Occasional annotations in French. Items arranged by subject country. Critic and subject indexes.

(B34) *Research Opportunities in Renaissance Drama.*

Lists current research projects in medieval drama.

(C3) *The Year's Work in Modern Language Studies.*

Medieval Latin studies are covered, Vol. 1—; Neo-Latin studies are covered, Vol. 32, 1970—.

(B33) *Seventeenth-Century News.*

"Neo-Latin News" in each issue, 1952—, lists summaries of recent books, articles, and dissertations.

(B35) *Studies in Philology.*

The Renaissance bibliography for years 1917–68 included studies of Renaissance Latin.

B25 *Bulletin de Philosophie Médiévale.* Louvain: International Soc. for the Study of Medieval Philosophy, 1959—. Annual.

Carries a list of new international translations and European editions of medieval texts.

B26 *Encomia.** Philadelphia: International Courtly Literature Soc., 1975—. Annual.

The Society's bibliographic annual, listing international books, reviews, and articles. Some annotations.

(D15) *Bulletin Bibliographique de la Société Internationale Arthurienne/ Bibliographical Bulletin of the International Arthurian Society.*

An annual, comprehensive, classified, and annotated bibliography of books and articles.

B. RENAISSANCE AND SEVENTEENTH CENTURY

The major Renaissance bibliography—the *Bibliographie Internationale de l'Humanisme et de la Renaissance*—is a comprehensive, international compilation of studies on all Renaissance literature and Renaissance subjects. *Renaissance Quarterly* has a less comprehensive but still valuable bibliography of current books on the Renaissance, and the *MLA International Bibliography* covers literary studies, although its coverage is spread over two volumes and, in English literature, over two sections. Other bibliographies provide more limited coverage of literature: the MHRA *Annual Bibliography*, *Seventeenth-Century News*, *The Year's Work in Modern Language Studies*, *The Year's Work in English Studies*, and *Studies in English Literature*. *Shakespearean Research and Opportunities* covers Elizabethan society in general, and several subject bibliographies listed in Chapter v should be of use (see especially the sections on art and aesthetics, history, libraries, science, and theology). Author bibliographies for Shakespeare, Cervantes, and Racine are also useful because of their broad coverage (see Ch. vi).

B30 *Bibliographie Internationale de l'Humanisme et de la Renaissance.* Geneva: Droz, 1966—. Annual.

An international, comprehensive, and classified bibliography for 1965—, of books and articles on all aspects of the European and Latin American Renaissance—history, religion and philosophy, the arts, literature and language, science and technology (each section has appropriate subdivisions), and individuals. Critic index. A less comprehensive version of this bibliography was carried for 1956–65 in *Bibliothèque d'Humanisme et Renaissance* (Paris: Droz, 1934—).

(A1) *MLA International Bibliography.*
Studies of English Renaissance literature are listed in Vol. I, English Literature, Section 6, Renaissance and Elizabethan, and Section 7, Seventeenth Century. Comparable coverage is provided in Vol. II for French, Italian, Spanish, German, Netherlands, and Scandinavian literatures. Comprehensive coverage of the period dates from the 1969 bibliography: before 1969 the major Renaissance literary bibliography appeared in *Studies in Philology.*

B31 *Renaissance Quarterly.* New York: Renaissance Soc. of America, 1948—. 4/yr.
(Titled *Renaissance News*, Vols. 1–19, 1946–66.)
"Renaissance Books," a classified list of international books on the fine arts, history, literature, and philosophy, religion, and science, appears in each issue, Vol. 5, 1952—.

B32 *Shakespearean Research and Opportunities.* New York: City Univ. of New York, 1965—. Irregular. Temporarily suspended, 1979—.
An international, classified, comprehensive, and annotated bibliography of books, articles, and dissertations on a great variety of Elizabethan and Renaissance intellectual issues, such as education, ethics, law, medicine, the arts, and theology.
These bibliographies have been collected: W.R. Elton and Giselle Neuschloss, *Shakespeare's World: Renaissance Intellectual Contexts. A Selective, Annotated Guide, 1966–71* (New York: Garland, 1979).

(B1) *Annual Bibliography of English Language and Literature.*
See chapters on 16th- and 17th-century literature.

(B2) *The Year's Work in English Studies.*
See chapters on the earlier 16th century, Shakespeare, English drama 1550–1660 (excluding Shakespeare), the later 16th century (excluding drama), the earlier 17th century (excluding drama), and Milton.

(B4) *Studies in English Literature, 1500–1900.*
See "Recent Studies in the English Renaissance" (winter) and "Recent Studies in Elizabethan and Jacobean Drama" (spring).

(C3) *The Year's Work in Modern Language Studies.*
Bibliographic essays cover work on Continental literatures.

B33 *Seventeenth-Century News.* University Park: Pennsylvania State Univ., 1941—. 4/yr.
Each issue carries abstracts of recent articles and dissertations on Milton, Donne, Jonson, Dryden, and other 17th-century English and American authors and literary subjects. A separate section provides similar coverage for Neo-Latin studies.

B34 *Research Opportunities in Renaissance Drama.* Lawrence: Univ. of Kansas, 1956—. Annual.
(Titled *Opportunities for Research in Renaissance Drama*, 1956–64.)
Lists current projects in Renaissance and medieval drama, chiefly but not exclusively in English. Also frequently publishes bibliographies on figures and subjects in Renaissance and medieval drama and an index to

these and to the "Current Projects" lists has been published: Christopher J. Thaiss, "An Index to Volumes I-XVI of *RORD*," *Research Opportunities in Renaissance Drama*, 17 (1974), 34–44.

B35 *Studies in Philology*. Chapel Hill: Univ. of North Carolina Press, 1906—. 5/yr.

Carried an annual, international, comprehensive, and classified bibliography of books and articles on the Renaissance for 1917–68 (in Vols. 14–66, 1917–69). Coverage of Continental literature and related subjects began with year 1938 (Vol. 36, 1939).

B36 *Quarterly Check-List of Renaissance Studies: An International Index of Current Books, Monographs, Brochures, and Separates*. Darien, Conn.: American Bibliographic Service, 1959–76. 4/yr.

An international author list of books on Renaissance subjects, with an annual author, editor, and translator index.

B37 *English Literary Renaissance*. Amherst: Univ. of Massachusetts, 1971—. 3/yr.

Each issue carries a bibliographic article on an English Renaissance figure, listing editions and studies on general issues, special topics, and individual works.

B38 *Elizabethan Bibliographies Supplements*. London: Nether, 1967—. Irregular.

Each issue is a bibliography of editions and studies for individual Elizabethan writers published from the 1930s to the late 1960s. Format and coverage vary from volume to volume.

Supplements: S. A. Tannenbaum and D. R. Tannenbaum, *Elizabethan Bibliographies*, 10 vols. (1937–50; rpt. Port Washington, N.Y.: Kennikat, 1967).

C. RESTORATION AND EIGHTEENTH CENTURY

The major bibliography of this period—*The Eighteenth Century: A Current Bibliography*—includes nonliterary subjects and non-English literatures (the latter from 1970). The MLA and MHRA bibliographies and *The Year's Work in English Studies* divide their coverage by century, so one must use both the seventeenth- and the eighteenth-century sections. *The Year's Work in Modern Language Studies* provides useful items about Continental literatures. There are no separate author bibliographies for English or American writers of this period, but both *Restoration* (B42) and *The Scriblerian and the Kit-Cats* (B43) provide some coverage of individual authors (see Ch. vi). See also the sections on history, libraries, journalism, science, theology, and women's studies in Chapter v.

B41 *The Eighteenth Century: A Current Bibliography*. New York: AMS, 1979—. Annual.

An international, comprehensive, classified bibliography of books and articles, 1924—, on all aspects of 18th-century life in Europe, Great Britain, and North America (and including the Restoration period in England). Covers history, society, economics, philosophy, science, religion, and fine arts as well as literature, printing, bibliography, and individual authors. The individual authors covered include several not primarily associated with literature, such as Hume, Kant, and Leibnitz. Each entry is annotated, the annotations for books being lengthy and evaluative. The bibliography for 1975 was published at Philadelphia by the American Society for Eighteenth-Century Studies, 1978; it was previously carried for 1924–74 in Vols. 5–54, 1926–75, of *Philological Quarterly* (Iowa City: Univ. of Iowa).

The bibliographies for 1925–69 have been collected: Ronald S. Crane and others, *English Literature 1660–1800: A Bibliography of Modern Studies*, 6 vols. (Princeton: Princeton Univ. Press, 1950–72).

(A1) *MLA International Bibliography.*

See the sections for 17th and 18th centuries under both English and American literature. Also see relevant sections in Vol. II.

(B1) *Annual Bibliography of English Language and Literature.*

See the sections for 17th and 18th centuries.

(B2) *The Year's Work in English Studies.*

See chapters for the Restoration and the 18th century and for American literature.

(C3) *The Year's Work in Modern Language Studies.*

See chapters on Continental literatures for the 17th and 18th centuries.

(B4) *Studies in English Literature, 1500–1900.*

See "Recent Studies in Restoration and Eighteenth Century" in the summer issue.

B42 *Restoration: Studies in English Literary Culture, 1660–1700.* Knoxville: Univ. of Tennessee, 1977—. 2/yr.

"Some Current Publications" in each issue is an annotated list of books, articles, and dissertations on English and American Restoration figures. Items are listed under subject authors, under general literature (with subdivisions for anthologies, editions, compilations, bibliographies, etc.), and general issues (history, philosophy, politics, religion, science, pedagogy, and other arts). Each issue also lists abstracts of recent papers.

B43 *The Scriblerian and the Kit-Cats.* Philadelphia: Temple Univ., 1969—. 2/yr.

(Titled *The Scriblerian: A Newsletter Devoted to Pope, Swift, and Their Circle*, 1969–71.)

Each issue consists of annotated lists of international books and articles on Pope, Swift, Dryden, the Kit-Cats, Defoe, Fielding, Richardson, and related figures and subjects. Items are arranged under "Foreign Reviews" and "Recent Studies." A subject and critic index, published every fifth year, is in effect a bibliography of studies of Restoration and early 18th-century English literature.

B44 *Restoration and Eighteenth Century Theatre Research.* Chicago: Loyola Univ., 1962—. 2/yr.

"Restoration and Eighteenth-Century Theatre Research Bibliography," for 1961—, is an annual, international, classified, and annotated list of books, articles, and dissertations, arranged by subject (for example, acting, sentimentalism, and names of playwrights and actors).

Bibliographies for 1961 through 1967 have been cumulated: Carl J. Stratman, ed., *Restoration and Eighteenth Century Theatre Research Bibliography 1961–1968* (Troy, N.Y.: Whitston, 1969).

B45 *Philological Quarterly.* Iowa City: Univ. of Iowa, 1922—. 4/yr.
Publishes four to six annual review articles that cover international
books and articles in Augustan and 18th-century studies.

D. ROMANTIC

There are two exemplary bibliographies for the Romantic Period, *The Romantic Movement: A Selective and Critical Bibliography* and the annual list in the
Keats-Shelley Journal. They are comprehensive, cover Continental Romanticism, the arts, politics, and social change, as well as literature, and they
have thorough subject classification or subject indexing. Coverage of the period
in the MLA and MHRA bibliographies and *The Year's Work in English Studies* is comprehensive but less conveniently arranged, with Romantics and
Pre-Romantics put in separate sections (Blake, for example, is listed as an
eighteenth-century writer). Several of the Romantics have individual author bibliographies (Ch. vi). See Chapter v for subject bibliographies. Pre-Romantics
and certain Romantic writers are also covered in *The Eighteenth Century: A
Current Bibliography* (B41).

B51 *The Romantic Movement: A Selective and Critical Bibliography.* New
York: Garland, 1980—. Annual.
An international, comprehensive, annotated bibliography of books,
reviews, articles, and dissertations on the English, French, German,
and Spanish Romantic movements. Arranged in three main sections: individual authors, the social, intellectual, political, and artistic environ-
ment, and bibliography. Previously, the bibliographies for 1964–78 were
carried in Vols. 3–17 of *English Language Notes* (Boulder: Univ. of Colorado, 1963–79), for 1949–63 in Vols. 29–43 of *Philological Quarterly*
(Iowa City: Univ. of Iowa, 1950–64), and for 1936–48 in Vols. 4–16 of
ELH: A Journal of English Literary History (Baltimore: Johns Hopkins
Univ. Press, 1937–49).
The Romantic bibliography has been collected: A. C. Elkins, Jr., and
L. J. Forstner, *The Romantic Movement Bibliography, 1936–1970,* 7
vols. (Ann Arbor: Pierian, 1973).

(A1) *MLA International Bibliography.*
See the sections on 18th- and 19th-century English literature in Vol. I,
and sections on Continental literatures in Vol. II.
(B1) *Annual Bibliography of English Language and Literature.*
See the sections on 18th- and 19th-century English literature.
(B2) *The Year's Work in English Studies.*
See chapters on the 18th and 19th centuries.
(C3) *The Year's Work in Modern Language Studies.*
See chapters on the Continental literatures.
B52 *Keats-Shelley Journal: Keats, Shelley, Byron, Hunt, and Their Circles.*
New York: Keats-Shelley Assn. of America, 1952—. Annual.
An annual, comprehensive, international bibliography of editions and
studies (books, reviews, articles) of the younger English Romantics—
Keats, Shelley, Byron, Hunt, Hazlitt, and their circles—and of Ro-
manticism in general. Most entries have a one-sentence annotation. Au-
thor, critic, and subject index.
The bibliographies for 1950–74 have been collected (but not cumulated): David B. Green and Edwin G. Wilson, eds., *Keats, Shelley, By-*

ron, Hunt, and Their Circles: A Bibliography: July 1, 1950–June 30, 1962 (Lincoln: Univ. of Nebraska Press, 1964), and Robert A. Hartley, ed., *Keats, Shelley, Byron, Hunt, and Their Circles: A Bibliography: July 1, 1962–December 31, 1974* (Lincoln: Univ. of Nebraska Press, 1978).

(B4) *Studies in English Literature, 1500–1900.*
See "Recent Studies in the Nineteenth Century" in the autumn issue.

E. VICTORIAN AND TRANSITION LITERATURE

In addition to the very comprehensive "Victorian Bibliography" in *Victorian Studies* and the *Annual Bibliography of Victorian Studies*, there are several valuable, specialized bibliographies on poetry, prose, periodicals, theater, and Transition figures, as well as the MLA and MHRA bibliographies and *The Year's Work in English Studies*. Because of the increasing interest in popular and sub-literary genres and subjects, several of the subject bibliographies in Chapter v will be of importance. See also the sections on American literature and Commonwealth literature in this chapter.

B54 *Victorian Studies.* Bloomington: Indiana Univ., 1957—. 4/yr.
"Victorian Bibliography" is an annual, international, comprehensive, classified list of books, reviews, articles, and dissertations on most aspects of the Victorian period in England. Literature, the arts, history, economics, education, religions, science, and sociology, as well as bibliography and studies on individual authors, are covered. The bibliography was formerly carried for years 1932–56 in Vols. 30–54 of *Modern Philology* (Chicago: Univ. of Chicago, 1933–57).
Cumulations: Ronald E. Freeman, ed., *Bibliographies of Victorian Literature for the Ten Years 1965–1974* (New York: AMS, 1981); Robert C. Slack, ed., *Bibliographies of Studies in Victorian Literature for the Ten Years 1955–1964* (Urbana: Univ. of Illinois Press, 1976); Austin Wright, ed., *Bibliographies of Studies in Victorian Literature for the Ten Years 1945–1954* (Urbana: Univ. of Illinois Press, 1956); and William D. Templeman, ed., *Bibliographies of Studies in Victorian Literature for the Thirteen Years 1932–1944* (Urbana: Univ. of Illinois Press, 1945).

B55 *Annual Bibliography of Victorian Studies.* Edmonton, Alberta: LTIR Database, 1980—. Annual.
Comprehensive, international bibliography of books, reviews, articles, and dissertations on the arts, philosophy and religion, social sciences, history, science and technology, and literature. Will cover years 1970—. Subject, title, and book reviewer indexes. Available for computerized searches.

(A1) *MLA International Bibliography.* See the section on 19th-century English literature.

(B1) *Annual Bibliography of English Language and Literature.*
See the section on 19th-century English literature.

(B2) *The Year's Work in English Studies.*
See the chapter on 19th-century English literature.

(B4) *Studies in English Literature, 1500–1900.*
See "Recent Studies in the Nineteenth Century" in the autumn issue.

B56 *Victorian Newsletter.* New York: New York Univ., 1952 —. 2/yr.
"Recent Publications. A Selected List" appears in each issue and lists books and articles on individual English authors, criticism and literary history, and bibliography.

B57 *Victorian Poetry: A Critical Journal of Victorian Literature.* Morgantown: West Virginia Univ., 1963—. 4/yr.
"Guide to the Year's Work in Victorian Poetry," 1962—, is a bibliographic essay on the year's international books and articles on poetry and, frequently, prose. Sections, written by different scholars, deal with general issues and individual authors.

B58 *Victorian Periodicals Review.* Toronto: Research Soc. for Victorian Periodicals, 1968—. 4/yr.
(Titled *Victorian Periodicals Newsletter*, 1968–78.)
"Victorian Periodicals [year]: A Checklist of Scholarship and Criticism," 1975—, is an annual list of North American and British books and articles on Victorian periodicals. Critic index.

(D315) *Prose Studies.*
Coverage includes Victorian nonfiction prose.

B59 *Nineteenth Century Theatre Research.* Tucson: Univ. of Arizona, 1973—. 2/yr.
"Nineteenth-Century Theatre Research: A Bibliography" is an annual, international list of books, articles, and dissertations about subjects (such as acting, audience, Australian theater) and persons. Critic index. A newsletter accompanying the journal, Vol. 1, 1977—, lists works in progress and items overlooked in the annual listing.

B60 *English Literature in Transition 1880–1920.* Tempe: Arizona State Univ., 1957—. 4/yr.
"Bibliography, News, and Notes," for 1956–74 (in Vol. 18, 1957–75), was an annual, international bibliography of books, reviews, and articles on Transition Period writers; articles and long reviews were annotated. Since 1975 the journal has published bibliographical articles on individual Transition figures.

F. TWENTIETH CENTURY

For research in twentieth-century literature the general humanities indexes, such as the *Arts and Humanities Citation Index* (A6) and the *Humanities Index* (A8), are especially helpful, as are the specialized bibliographies for Transition and Modernist literature. See also sections in Chapter v on children's literature, comparative literature, creative writing (mainly North American writers), film, little magazines, popular culture, science fiction, women's studies, and the literary genres. Author bibliographies are listed in Chapter vi.

(A1) *MLA International Bibliography.*
See the sections on English, Commonwealth, and American literatures.

(B1) *Annual Bibliography of English Language and Literature.*
See the chapter on 20th-century English, American, and Commonwealth literature.

(B2) *The Year's Work in English Studies.*
The chapter on 20th-century literature includes English and Commonwealth literature. A separate chapter covers American literature.

(B60) *English Literature in Transition 1880–1920.*
  An annual bibliography of Transition figures covered years 1956–74.
B65 *Journal of Modern Literature.* Philadelphia: Temple Univ., 1970—.
  4/yr.
  Carries an annual, international, comprehensive, classified bibliography of English language scholarship on modernist writers (1885–1950), with an emphasis on Anglo-American figures. Covers books, articles, dissertations, symposia and special numbers, and miscellaneous information (such as library holdings, conferences, important sales). Categories include bibliography, literary history, themes and movements, comparison studies, criticism, film as literature, and individual writers. Author and critic index.
B66 *Twentieth Century Literature: A Scholarly and Critical Journal.* Hempstead, N.Y.: Hofstra Univ. Press, 1955—. 4/yr.
  Each issue carries an international, annotated list of articles on 20th-century writers. Items are listed by subject (such as American fiction, criticism, Marxism) and by subject author.
  The bibliographies for 1954–70 have been augmented and cumulated: David Pownall, *Articles on Twentieth Century Literature: An Annotated Bibliography.* 8 vols. (New York: Kraus-Thomson, 1973–82).
(D151) *Modern Drama.*
  Carries an annual bibliography of studies on international 20th-century drama and dramatists.
B67 *Contemporary Literary Criticism: Excerpts from Criticism of the Works of Today's Novelists, Poets, Playwrights, and Other Creative Writers.* Detroit: Gale, 1973—. 2/yr.
  Selective excerpts of English-language books and articles on contemporary figures (mainly British and American, living or who have died after 1959). Beginning with Vol. 12 *CLC* coverage includes songwriters, filmmakers, cartoonists, screenwriters, and producers, as well as writers. Cumulative author and critic indexes in each volume.

3. AMERICAN LITERATURE

The general bibliographies and periodical indexes listed in Chapter ii cover American literature; one should use them as well as the MLA and MHRA bibliographies, *Abstracts of English Studies*, and relevant period bibliographies. Many of the subject bibliographies in Chapter v are essential. See, for example, American studies, black studies, children's literature, ethnic studies, film, little magazines, popular culture, regionalism, science fiction, women's studies, and the literary genres. *The Year's Work in English Studies* offers a corrective—or at least a stimulating alternative—to Americans' view of their own literature, and it, along with *American Literary Scholarship*, not only reviews and evaluates the year's criticism but also comments on such matters as the state of editions, manuscripts, archives, and bibliography. Most of the major, and many minor, authors have author bibliographies (see Ch. vi).

(A1) *MLA International Bibliography.*
  The American literature section of Vol. I is subdivided into pre-1800 figures and concerns, 1800–70, 1870–1900, and the 20th century. Each

section lists scholarship on genres, individual authors, and such distinctly American issues as Afro-American literature.

B71 *American Literature: A Journal of Literary History, Criticism and Bibliography.* Durham, N.C.: Duke Univ. Press, 1929—. 4/yr.

"Articles on American Literature Appearing in Current Periodicals," a selective list of articles on major authors and general issues, appears in each issue, Vol. 1, No. 3—, 1929—. Dissertations and other works in progress are listed separately.

The bibliographic lists have been cumulated and augmented: Lewis Leary, comp., with John Auchard, *Articles on American Literature, 1968–1975* (Durham, N.C.: Duke Univ. Press, 1979);———, comp., with Carolyn Bartholet and Catherine Roth, *Articles on American Literature 1950–1967* (Durham, N.C.: Duke Univ. Press, 1970); and ———, *Articles on American Literature 1900–1950* (Durham, N.C.: Duke Univ. Press, 1954).

(B1) *Annual Bibliography of English Language and Literature.*

Books, reviews, articles, and dissertations on American authors are included with those on British writers and are arranged by period.

B72 *American Literary Scholarship: An Annual.* Durham, N.C.: Duke Univ. Press, 1965—. Annual.

Evaluative bibliographic essays by noted scholars on the year's work in American literature, for 1963—. Arranged in two parts, the first with chapters on individual major authors, the second with chapters on periods, genres, and related subjects (variously folklore, 1963–74; black literature, 1975—; foreign scholarship, 1974—; and themes, topics, and criticism, 1966—). The chapters on individual authors comment on editions, bibliographical materials, biographical studies, and criticism (books and articles); the other chapters note general studies, and the chapter on themes, topics, and criticism is a particularly useful survey of trends in American literary theory. No subject index; author and critic indexes.

(B2) *The Year's Work in English Studies.*

Studies on American literature are now surveyed in two chapters.

(D1) *American Quarterly.*

Carried an annual list of articles on American studies, 1954–72.

(B33) *Seventeenth-Century News.*

"Americana Abstracts" is a list of abstracts of current articles on 17th-century American literature.

(B41) *The Eighteenth Century: A Current Bibliography.*

Includes books and articles on American literature and individual authors of the 18th century.

(B65) *Journal of Modern Literature.*

The annual bibliography on Modernism includes American authors, 1885–1950.

(B66) *Twentieth Century Literature.*

The quarterly list of articles, with abstracts, includes studies on 20th-century American authors.

(D151) *Modern Drama.*

The annual bibliography includes 20th-century American dramatists.

(B67) *Contemporary Literary Criticism.*

Coverage includes studies of contemporary (post-1960) American authors.

4. COMMONWEALTH LITERATURE

The Commonwealth literatures are adequately covered in the major comprehensive bibliographies and *Abstracts of English Studies*, but one should also consult the more specialized items listed here as well as the appropriate bibliographies in the sections for African and Asian literatures (Ch. iv).

A. GENERAL COMMONWEALTH
  (A1) *MLA International Bibliography.*
      Studies on Australian, Canadian, and the English language literatures of Africa, Sri Lanka, India, Malaysia, Malta, New Zealand, Oceania, Philippines, South Africa, and the West Indies are listed in Vol. I under English literature.
  (B1) *Annual Bibliography of English Language and Literature.*
      Commonwealth writers in English are included in the century-by-century coverage.
  (B2) *The Year's Work in English Studies.*
      Includes selective coverage of Commonwealth writers in English.
  B75 *Journal of Commonwealth Literature.* Oxford: Hans Zell, 1965—. 3/yr.
      The "Annual Bibliography of Commonwealth Literature," for 1964–, is an international, classified bibliography of creative writing, belles lettres, and criticism (books and articles) on individual authors and the literature of various Commonwealth countries.
  (D266) *Index to Commonwealth Little Magazines.*
      Coverage includes critical and bibliographical articles and book reviews.
  (B65) *Journal of Modern Literature.*
      An annual bibliography, 1974—, includes Commonwealth writers of 1885–1950.
  (B66) *Twentieth Century Literature.*
      Quarterly bibliography covers 20th-century Commonwealth writers.
  (D151) *Modern Drama.*
      Annual bibliography includes 20th-century Commonwealth dramatists.
  (B67) *Contemporary Literary Criticism.*
      Coverage includes contemporary Commonwealth writers.

B. AUSTRALIA
  B76 *Australian Literary Studies.* St. Lucia: Univ. of Queensland Press, 1963—. 2/yr.
      Carries an annual list of international books and articles on Australian literary figures, works, and subjects.
  B77 *Pinpointer: A Current Guide to Popular Periodicals.* Adelaide: Libraries Board of South Australia, 1963—. 6/yr.
      Author and subject index to general-interest Australian periodicals, although with relatively little coverage of literature.
  B78 *Index to Australian Book Reviews.* Adelaide: Libraries Board of South Australia, 1965–. 4/yr.
      Indexes book reviews carried in Australian journals of books by Australians, published in Australia, or of Australian interest. Emphasizes books in literature, humanities, and social sciences.

C. CANADA

B80 *Journal of Canadian Fiction.* Guelph, Ont., and Montreal: Journal of Canadian Fiction, 1972—. 4/yr.

"Canadian Literature: An Annotated Bibliography/Literature Canadienne: Une Bibliographie avec Commentaire" is an annual, international, classified list of books, reviews, articles, and dissertations on all aspects of Canadian literature. French subjects and figures are interfiled with English, and creative writing and scholarly tools, critical studies, and reviews of books, films, and theater are included. Author and critic index.

B81 *University of Toronto Quarterly.* Toronto: Univ. of Toronto, 1932—. 4/yr.

"Letters in Canada" is an annual, evaluative bibliographic essay surveying the year's creative writing, for 1935—, in fiction, poetry, drama, and belles lettres. Covers both French and English writing and includes a section on work in other languages. Author index to the books surveyed.

B82 *The Annotated Bibliography of Canada's Major Authors.* Downsview, Ont.: ECW, 1979—. Irregular.

Each volume provides an international, comprehensive, primary, and secondary bibliography of Canada's French- and English-language authors, through 1978. Updating supplements will be issued irregularly.

(D80) *Canadian Review of Comparative Literature/Revue Canadienne de Littérature Comparée.*

Carries an annual supplement to its "Preliminary Bibliography of Comparative Canadian Literature," 1976—.

B83 *Canadian Literature.* Vancouver: Univ. of British Columbia, 1959—. 4/yr.

"Canadian Literature," 1959–70 (in Nos. 7–48, 1960–71), was an annual list of the year's critical and creative writing by and about Canadians in French and English, during an important decade in the history of Canadian literature.

B84 *Canadian Periodical Index.* Ottawa: Canadian Library Assn., 1928—. 12/yr.

(Formerly titled *Canadian Index to Periodicals*, 1948–63, and *Canadian Periodical Index*, 1928–47.)

An author and subject index to general-interest Canadian periodicals.

(A13) *Canadian Essay and General Literature Index.*

Indexed festschriften and collective volumes published in Canada on all subjects.

B85 *Canadian Book Review Annual.* Toronto: PMA Books, 1975—. Annual.

Brief evaluative reviews of Canadian English-language books are listed in five classes: reference, humanities and fine arts, literature, social sciences, and science and technology. Author, title, and subject indexes. Literature covered includes novels, short stories, poetry, drama, criticism, folklore, mythology, and children's literature. Humanities includes language, linguistics and philosophy, theater, cinema, and radio and television.

28   *Commonwealth Literature*

D. OTHER
    B88 *Index to New Zealand Periodicals.* Wellington: National Library of New
         Zealand, 1941—. Annual.
    B89 *Index to South African Periodicals/Repertorium van Suid-Afrikaanse
         Tydskrifartikels.* Johannesburg: Public Library, 1940—. Annual.

Chapter Four.   Non-English Literatures

For most North American scholars in the non-English language literatures the *MLA International Bibliography* (A1) and *The Year's Work in Modern Language Studies* (C3) will be the first bibliographies to turn to simply because the items cited in them are likely to be available in their libraries. There are, however, more specialized and more comprehensive bibliographies for many of these literatures. One should consult other general literary bibliographies (especially the *Bulletin Signalétique*, A2, and *LLINQUA: Language and Literature Index Quarterly*, A3), the bibliographies for national literatures (such as the *Bibliographie der französischen Literaturwissenschaft*, C11), general and humanities periodical indexes (A6–A27), and relevant period, subject, and author bibliographies. The most comprehensive bibliographies for literary periods are listed in Chapter iii and cross-referenced from appropriate sections of this chapter. Linguistics and language bibliographies are listed in Chapter v.

The divisions in this chapter follow those in the *MLA International Bibliography*, Vol. II.

1.   GENERAL ROMANCE LITERATURE

(A1)   *MLA International Bibliography*.
Covers studies in all the Romance literatures.

C1   *Romanische Bibliographie/Bibliographie Romane/Romance Bibliography*. Tübingen: Niemeyer, 1965—. Annual.
An international, comprehensive, and classified bibliography of books, reviews, and articles on linguistics and literature of all the Romance languages, including non-European ones (for example, Canadian and Louisianan French and Cape Verdean Portuguese). In three parts: Part I has author, subject, and book review indexes for Parts I, II, and III; Part II covers linguistics; Part III covers literature, with sections for bibliographic and general studies and then for studies arranged by nation, subdivided for individual authors and subjects. Coverage dates from 1875, starting with its predecessor, *Zeitschrift für romanische Philologie*. *Supplementheft* (Tübingen: Niemeyer, 1878–1964).

C2   *Romanistisches Jahrbuch*. Berlin: de Gruyter, 1947—. Annual.
Lists current *habilitationsschriften* and dissertations on Romance languages and literatures written at West German and Austrian universities, for 1945—.

C3   *The Year's Work in Modern Language Studies*. London: Modern Humanities Research Assn., 1931—. Annual.

An evaluative survey by noted scholars of the year's international books and articles, 1930—, on modern European non-English literatures. After a chapter discussing general linguistics studies, there are major chapters for medieval and Neo-Latin, Romance (including South American), Germanic (including Netherlandic and Scandinavian), Celtic, and Slavonic literatures, with each chapter having subsections for language studies and for specific literatures and literary periods. Within the last are further subdivisions for genres and individual writers. Not every issue, however, has complete coverage of all the languages and literatures listed. Author, subject, and critic indexes. The subject indexing, an outstanding feature since Vol. 30, 1968, includes such headings as fables, the Fall, fascism, Faust theme, F.B.I., feminism, folklore.

C4   *Revue des Langues Romanes*. Montpellier: Centre d'Étude Occitanes de l'Université, 1870—. 2/yr.

"Bibliographie des Études Romanes en Amerique du Nord," 1968—, is a classified checklist of North American scholarship (chiefly books) on the Romance languages and literatures, arranged by country and literary period.

C5   *Romania*. Paris: Lecoy, 1872—. 4/yr.

Carries an international bibliography of current articles on Romance languages and literatures.

C6   *Modern Language Journal*. Madison: Univ. of Wisconsin Press, 1916—. 4/yr.

"American Doctoral Degrees Granted in Foreign Languages," 1925—, lists current degree recipients and titles of dissertations.

C7   *Revue de Linguistique Romane*. Strasbourg: Société de Linguistique Romane, 1925—. 2/yr.

"Chronique Bibliographique," Vol. 17— (1950—), is a classified list of reviews of recent international books on Romance linguistics.

2.   FRENCH AND FRANCOPHONE LITERATURE

See the list of general Romance bibliographies in the previous section.

French literary studies are served by several excellent general bibliographies that are listed here in order of their general availability and comprehensiveness. The *MLA International Bibliography* and the *Bibliographie der französischen Literaturwissenschaft* are similar in coverage, but the former provides better access to North American journals and books and is, therefore, more readily usable in the U.S.A. In contrast, the latter not only lists more French publications but also is more varied and thorough in listing studies of subjects related to French literature, like film and French culture. Other important bibliographies are the annual *Romanische Bibliographie* and *Bibliographie de la Littérature Française de Moyen Age à Nos Jours*, the bimonthly *Revue d'Histoire Littéraire de la France*, and the annual bibliographic survey in *The Year's Work in Modern Language Studies*. These general bibliographies include Francophone literature.

In addition, fairly good coverage of French literary periods is provided by the major period bibliographies listed in Chapter iii; these are listed here with abbreviated annotations. Bibliographies of dissertations on French literature and linguistics are included here. Author bibliographies are listed in Chapter vi. The subject bibliographies for art and aesthetics, Arthurian studies, comparative literature, critical and literary theory, film, linguistics and language, music, science fiction, and the literary genres should be useful (Ch. v). Also see the listings under general literary bibliographies and humanities periodical indexes in Chapter ii.

A. GENERAL BIBLIOGRAPHIES

(A1) *MLA International Bibliography.*

Studies are listed by period, within which are subdivisions for genres, topics (for example, *decadentisme* in the 19th-century section), and individual authors. French Canadians are in a separate section.

(A2) *Bulletin Signalétique 523.*

Coverage of French literature and French publications is especially good.

C11 *Bibliographie der französischen Literaturwissenschaft.* Frankfurt am Main: Klostermann, 1960—. Annual.

An international, comprehensive, and classified bibliography of books, reviews, articles, and dissertations, for 1956—, on French literature and related subjects, with critic, author, and subject indexes. French language items predominate, and editorial matter is in French. Sections: generalities (for example, culture and civilization, structuralism, cinema, stylistics and rhetoric), literary periods (with subdivisions for appropriate subjects, such as Chanson de geste, Encyclopédie, and Surréalisme et Dada), French-language literatures outside France, and individual authors.

(C1) *Romanische Bibliographie.*

Provides comprehensive coverage of international scholarship on French literature.

(C3) *The Year's Work in Modern Language Studies.*

The annual bibliographic essay on international scholarship reviews scholarly tools and new editions as well as criticism and is subdivided for language studies, studies on the literary periods, and Provençal studies.

C12 *Bibliographie de la Littérature Française du Moyen Age à Nos Jours.* Paris: Colin, 1967—. Annual.

(Former titles: *Bibliographie de la Littérature Française Moderne (XVI-XXᵉ Siècles)*, 1962–65; *Bibliographie Littérature*, 1953–61; *Revue d'Histoire Littéraire de la France*, 1949–51.)

An international, comprehensive, and classified bibliography of books, articles, and dissertations, for 1948—. Arrangement: bibliographies, generalities, and periods or centuries, and within the last are subsections for general studies, themes, and individual writers. There are indexes for authors, subjects, and principal themes.

Coverage from 1949 to 1963 duplicated that in the *Revue d'Histoire Littéraire de la France*, but now the coverage is separate and more extensive.

C13 *Revue d'Histoire Littéraire de la France.* Paris: La Société d'Histoire Littéraire de la France, 1894—. 6/yr.

Each bimonthly issue carries a list of current scholarship, arranged by century (16th to 20th) and then by subject and subject author. Covers books, articles, pamphlets, and dissertations about literature and literary history. No index; no annual cumulation, but the lists for 1963—are available separately from the publisher. See the previous entry for information about the 1949–63 cumulations.

C14   *Bulletin Critique du Livre Français.* Paris: Association pour la Diffusion de la Pensée Française, 1945—. 11/yr.

A monthly list of brief reviews of French books in all subjects, including translations into French. The literature section includes criticism and creative writing. Author and title indexes in each issue and cumulated annually.

C15   *Bulletin Analytique de Linguistique Française.* Paris: Didier, 1970—. 6/yr.

A bimonthly, international, classified bibliography of books, articles, and dissertations on French linguistics, with brief annotations in French. Bimonthly author index cumulates annually.

C16   *Periodex.* Quebec: La Centrale des Bibliotheques, 1972—. 12/yr.

Subject index to about 90 French-language periodicals in all subjects.

C17   *French Review.* Champaign, Ill.: American Assn. of Teachers of French, 1927—. 4/yr.

"Dissertations in Progress," 1963—, is an annual list of current North American dissertations, arranged by subject.

C18   *French Periodical Index.* Boston: Faxon, 1976—. Annual.

A classified index to ten general-interest French-language periodicals. Relevant sections are films, literature, books, libraries, publishing, and theater.

C19   *Current Research in French Studies at Universities and University Colleges in the United Kingdom.* Sheffield: Soc. for French Studies, 1969—. Annual.

A classified list of U. K. theses and research in progress, arranged in sections for literary periods, linguistics, and Francophone studies. The critic index has an elaborate code indicating the researcher's institution, the nature of the research, and whether the research has been completed or abandoned.

B.   FRENCH LITERARY PERIODS

See Chapter iii for complete annotations of the general period bibliographies for English and European literatures.

Medieval

(B15)   *International Medieval Bibliography.*

Use the index to find books, articles, and notes on French medieval literature and culture.

(B16)   *Cahiers de Civilisation Médiévale X^e-XIIe Siècles: Bibliographie.*

Items are accessible through a subject and proper-name index.

Renaissance

(B30)   *Bibliographie International de l'Humanisme et de la Renaissance.*

A classified, comprehensive, international bibliography of books and articles.

C21   *French 17: An Annual Descriptive Bibliography of French Seventeenth-Century Studies.* Fort Collins: Colorado State Univ., 1953—. Annual.

Published for the Seventeenth-Century French Division of the Modern Language Association, this international, comprehensive, and classified bibliography lists books, reviews, articles, and dissertations, Five sections: Bibliography and Linguistics, Political and Social Philosophy, Science and Religion, Literary History and Criticism, and Authors and Personages. Brief annotations.

C22 *Oeuvres & Critiques: Revue International d'Étude de la Reception Critique des Oeuvres Littéraires Française.* Paris: Place, 1976—. 2/yr.

"North American Publications on French Seventeenth-Century Literature" culls studies from *French 17* (C21) and arranges them under the subject author.

"North American Research in Progress on Seventeenth Century French Literature" lists dissertation topics by subject and research projects by critic (latter has a subject index). "North American Doctoral Theses on Seventeenth Century French Literature Completed [year]" lists items by genre or subject author.

Enlightenment
(B41) *The Eighteenth Century: A Current Bibliography.*
Coverage of French literature began with the 1970 bibliography. All aspects of 18th-century culture are covered.

Romanticism and Nineteenth Century
(B51) *The Romantic Movement: A Selective and Critical Bibliography.*
This annual, comprehensive, international, and annotated bibliography lists work on individual authors as well as on social, intellectual, political, and artistic aspects of European Romantic culture.

C23 *French VI Bibliography: Critical and Biographical References for the Study of Nineteenth Century French Literature.* New York: French Inst. and the Modern Language Assn., 1955–69. Annual.
An international, classified bibliography for 1954–67 of books, reviews, articles, and dissertations. Subject index.

Twentieth Century
C24 *French XX Bibliography.* New York: French Inst. and the Modern Language Assn., 1949—. Annual.
(Formerly *French VII Bibliography: Critical and Biographical References for the Study of Contemporary French Literature.* New York: Stechert-Hafner, 1949–58.)
A comprehensive, classified, international bibliography of books, articles, and newspaper stories (selective), for 1940—. Arranged in three parts: Part I covers general aspects, bibliographies, literary genres, aesthetics, themes, literary history, philosophy, religion, surrealism, symbolism, and theater; Part II covers individual authors and lists editions and studies; Part III covers cinema.

(B65) *Journal of Modern Literature.*
Carries an annual, comprehensive bibliography of English language books and articles on Modernist literary figures, 1885–1950. Although mainly concerned with Anglo-American writers, significant French writers of the period are covered.

(B66)   *Twentieth Century Literature*.
        Carries a quarterly, annotated list of articles on 20th-century writers.
(D151) *Modern Drama*
        Carries an annual bibliography on 20th-century dramatists.
  C25   *La Revue des Lettres Modernes: Histoire des Idées et des Littératures*.
        Paris: Minard, 1954—. Irregular.
        An extensive critical series on 20th-century French writing, with sub-series devoted to a number of individual authors. During the 1960s and early 1970s nearly every issue (made up of several numbers) carried a bibliography of editions, books, and articles, but more recently the regularity of these bibliographies has diminished. These writers have sub-series: Apollinaire, Barbey d'Aurevilly, Beckett, Bernanos, Camus, Céline, Claudel, Cocteau, Gide, Giono, Jacob, Malraux, Mauriac, Rimbaud, Suarès, Valéry, Verne.

3.   ITALIAN LITERATURE

After the *MLA International Bibliography*, the major Italian bibliography is the one carried in *La Rassegna della Letteratura Italiana*, which is international in coverage but puts special emphasis on Italian scholarship. There are two lists of North American studies (in *Italica* and *Revue des Langues Romanes*) and one of British studies (in *Italian Studies*). *The Year's Work in Modern Language Studies* provides comprehensive bibliographic essays on the year's international scholarship, as does *Lettere Italiane*, although to a lesser extent and from an Italian point of view.

Of the major period bibliographies listed in Chapter iii, the ones that are important for students of Italian literature are included below. Author bibliographies are listed in Chapter vi, subject bibliographies in Chapter v (see the sections for art and aesthetics, comparative literature, film, linguistics and language, music, and the literary genres, among others), and general humanities periodical indexes in Chapter ii.

The bibliographies here are listed in order of their comprehensiveness and general availability in North American libraries.

A.   GENERAL BIBLIOGRAPHIES
  (A1) *MLA International Bibliography*.
        International studies (books, articles, and dissertations) on Italian literature are arranged in six sections: General and Miscellaneous; Dante; Thirteenth and Fourteenth Centuries: Fifteenth, Sixteenth, and Seventeenth Centuries; Eighteenth and Nineteenth Centuries; and Twentieth Century.
  C31   *La Rassegna della Letteratura Italiana*. Florence: Sansoni, 1893—. 3/yr.
        Each issue carries an international, classified, comprehensive, and annotated bibliography of books, reviews, and articles on Italian literature. Arranged by literary period (*Trecento, Quattrocento, Cinquecento, Settecento*, etc.) and includes a section of Dante studies. Annotations are in Italian and are often extensive.
  (C1) *Romanische Bibliographie*.
        Part III, subdivided by nation, lists international books and articles on Italian literature and individual writers.

(C3) *The Year's Work in Modern Language Studies.*
Italian language and literature studies are covered in a single chapter, subdivided by literary periods.

C32 *Italica.* New Brunswick, N.J.: American Assn. of Teachers of Italian, 1924—. 4/yr.
A quarterly "Bibliography of Italian Studies in North America," 1923—, lists books, reviews, articles, and bibliographies on general, pedagogical, and Italian-American studies, with studies of Italian literature arranged by century. Items listed have been published in North America or abroad by North American scholars; subjects covered include comparative literature, translations, art, music, philosophy, history, film, and sociology (if relevant to literary issues).

C33 *Studi e Problemi di Critica Testuale.* Bologna: Casa de Risparmio, 1970—. 2/yr.
"American Bibliography" is an annual checklist of articles in American journals and of American reviews of books on Italian literature, film, theater, and arts. In addition there is an annotated bibliography of Italian books and articles on literature and philology in general.

(C4) *Revue des Langues Romanes.*
Includes an annual list of North American books and articles on Romance literatures, including Italian.

C34 *Italian Studies: An Annual Review.* Cambridge: Soc. for Italian Studies, 1937—. Annual.
A classified, selective bibliography of books and articles published in Great Britain on Italian studies in general. Note the sections on language and on literature and philosophy; the latter section includes mention of current creative writing (including translations) and studies on comparative literature, especially those linking Italy and Great Britain.

C35 *Lettere Italiane.* Florence: Olschki, 1949—. 4/yr.
The quarterly "Rassegna," a bibliographic essay, reviews recent criticism on Italian writers or literary subjects.

B. LITERARY PERIODS

Except for coverage provided by the general Italian literature bibliographies just described, there seem to be no specialized period bibliographies. The following, however, do provide useful coverage of Italian literature.

Medieval
(B15) *International Medieval Bibliography.*
See also other medieval bibliographies listed with the *IMB*.

Renaissance
(B30) *Bibliographie Internationale de l'Humanisme et de la Renaissance.*

Eighteenth Century
(B41) *The Eighteenth Century: A Current Bibliography.*
Coverage of all aspects of 18th-century Italian culture began with the 1970 bibliography.

Romanticism

(B51) *The Romantic Movement: A Selective and Critical Bibliography.*
Coverage of studies on Italian literature has been spotty. See years
1936–42, 1953–72, 1976, and 1978.

Twentieth Century

(B65) *Journal of Modern Literature.*
Carries an annual bibliography on Modernist writers, 1885–1950.

(B66) *Twentieth Century Literature.*
Carries an annotated list of articles on international 20th-century
writers in each issue.

(D151) *Modern Drama.*
Carries an annual bibliography of studies on 20th-century
dramatists.

4.   SPANISH AND PORTUGUESE LITERATURE

The *MLA International Bibliography* and the *Romanische Bibliographie*, un-
like the extensive bibliographies in *Nueva Revista de Filología Hispánica*, have
the great virtue of covering both peninsular and Latin American Spanish and
Portuguese writing. Other Latin American bibliographies are listed in Section B
below. Among the useful subject bibliographies in Chapter v are those for American studies, black studies, comparative literature, the Don Juan theme, ethnic
studies, film, linguistics and language, and the literary genres. Author bibliographies are listed in Chapter vi, and general humanities indexes in Chapter ii.
The bibliographies are listed here in order of their comprehensiveness and
general availability in North American libraries.

A.   GENERAL BIBLIOGRAPHIES

(A1) *MLA International Bibliography.*
Contains sections for Spanish, Portuguese, and Brazilian studies,
with Spanish being further subdivided: General and Miscellaneous,
Spanish American to 1930 and since 1930, Spanish Literature before
1500, 1500–1700, Eighteenth and Nineteenth Centuries, and the Twentieth Century. Spanish literature was covered from the beginning of the
bibliography; Spanish American coverage was added with year 1926;
Portuguese (including Brazilian) literature was added in 1928; and Brazilian literature was given a separate section in 1938.

(C1) *Romanische Bibliographie.*
Coverage includes all the Portuguese and Spanish language literatures.

C41 *Nueva Revista de Filología Hispánica.* México: El Colegio de México,
1947— . 2/yr.
Each issue carries an international, comprehensive, and classified bibliography of books, reviews, articles, and dissertations on peninsular
Spanish and Portuguese linguistics, literature, and related bibliographic
and historical studies; coverage began for the early 1940s. The literature
section has subdivisions for the national literatures, themes, theory and
criticism, and genres. Coverage here was preceded by that in *Revista de
Filología Hispánica* (Buenos Aires: Universidad Nacional, 1939–46).

C42 *Revista de Filología Española.* Madrid: Consejo Superior de Investigaciones Científicas, 1914— . 4/yr.

Carries an annual, international, classified bibliography of books, reviews, and articles, 1913—, on Spanish linguistics and Spanish and Spanish American literature.

(C3) *The Year's Work in Modern Language Studies.*
Contains separate bibliographic essays on current, international books and articles on Spanish, Catalan, Portuguese, and Latin American language and literature.

(C4) *Revue des Langues Romanes.*
Lists North American studies on Spanish and other Romance languages and literatures.

C43 *Revista de Dialectología y Tradiciones Populares.* Madrid: Consejo Superior de Investigaciones Científicas, 1944—. 4/yr.
Carries an annual, international, classified bibliography of books and articles, 1948—, on linguistics and dialectology and on folklore, music, and religion, chiefly in Spain and Spanish-speaking America.

C44 *Hispania: A Journal Devoted to the Interests of the Teaching of Spanish and Portuguese.* Worcester, Mass.: American Assn. of Teachers of Spanish and Portuguese, 1918—. 5/yr.
"Dissertations in the Hispanic Languages and Literatures," 1935—, is an annual author list of North American dissertations completed or in progress.
"Research Tools in Progress," a subsection of "Professional News" and in each issue 1978—, reports on bibliographies, editions, concordances, and other scholarly tools for language and literature study.

C45 *Boletim Internacional de Bibliografia Luso-Brasileira.* Lisbon: Fundação Calouste Gulbenkian, 1960—. 4/yr.
"Registo Bibliográfico" lists new books and articles published in or about Portugal and Brazil. The literature section is further subdivided for creative writing and literary studies. Appeared quarterly in Vols. 1–12, annually in Vol. 13—.

(C6) *Modern Language Journal.*
"American Doctoral Degrees Granted in Foreign Languages," 1925—, lists current degree recipients and titles of dissertations.

B. LATIN AMERICAN LITERATURE

C48 *Chasqui: Revista de Literatura Latinoamericana.* Williamsburg, Va.: College of William and Mary, 1971—. 3/yr.
Each issue carries a list of current criticism and essays on Latin American literature and, selectively, current creative writing.

C49 *Handbook of Latin American Studies.* Gainesville: Univ. of Florida Press, 1936—. Annual.
A selective and annotated bibliography of recent publications in literature and the humanities (art, history, language, music, and philosophy) appears every other year, alternating with a bibliography of studies in the social sciences. Humanities and social sciences studies were combined in each annual, Volumes 1–26; humanities and literature are now in the even numbered volumes, 28, 30, 32, etc. Brazilian, Spanish American, and French West Indian literature is covered, and creative writing is listed as well as criticism; all items are annotated.

C50 *Bibliographic Guide to Latin American Studies.* Boston: Hall, 1979—. Annual.

An international, comprehensive bibliography, for 1978—, of books, serials, and other separate publications cataloged by the Library of Congress and the New York Public Library. Items are arranged by author, title, and subject.

C51   *Revista Interamericana de Bibliografía: Organo de Estudios Humanísticos/Interamerican Review of Bibliography: Journal of Humanistic Studies.* Washington, D.C.: Organization of American States, 1951—. 4/yr.

Each issue carries a selective, international, classified list of books on Latin American subjects acquired by the OAS and other libraries. See the sections on literature, art, music and dance, philosophy and psychology, and religion.

C52   *Hispanic American Periodicals Index.* Los Angeles: UCLA Latin American Center Publications, 1977—. Annual.

An author and subject index to over 200 international scholarly periodicals of Latin American interest, 1975—. Covers the humanities and social sciences and includes creative writing, criticism, and reviews of books, plays, and films.

C53   *A Guide to Reviews of Books from and about Hispanic America/Guía a las reseñas de libros de y sobre Hispanoamérica.* Detroit: Blaine Ethridge, 1976—. Annual.

An international, annotated index to reviews. Arranged by author, with title and subject indexes. Formerly published in Rio Piedras, Puerto Rico, in 1965 for years 1960–64, and in 1973 for 1965.

C54   *Caribbean Studies.* Rio Piedras: Univ. of Puerto Rico, 1961—. 4/yr.

"Current Bibliography" lists books and articles published in or about the Caribbean nations. Two issues are devoted to the island nations and two to the circum-Caribbean nations.

C55   *Cuban Studies/Estudios Cubanos.* Pittsburgh: Univ. of Pittsburgh, 1970—. 2/yr.

(Titled *Cuban Studies Newsletter*, 1970.)

"Classified Bibliography" is an annual, international list of books, pamphlets, and articles on all aspects of Cuba. See the section on language and literature.

C.   LITERARY PERIODS

The only exclusively Spanish period bibliography is that carried in the *Bulletin of the Comediantes* (C57), but the major period bibliographies listed in Chapter iii include studies of Spanish and Portuguese literature.

Medieval

(B15)   *International Medieval Bibliography.*

Renaissance

(B30)   *Bibliographie Internationale d'Humanisme et de la Renaissance.*

C57   *Bulletin of the Comediantes.* Los Angeles: Univ. of Southern California, 1948—. 2/yr.

"Bibliography of Publications on the Comedia" is an annual, international bibliography of books, articles, dissertations, and reviews on Spanish drama and dramatists of the Golden Age. First issued as a supplement to the 1950 volume and covering only non–North American items, the bibliography now includes North American publications (Vol. 26, 1974—).

Eighteenth Century

(B41) *The Eighteenth Century: A Current Bibliography.*
Coverage of studies of Continental literatures began with the 1970 bibliography.

Romanticism

(B51) *The Romantic Movement: A Selective and Critical Bibliography.*
Covers Spanish literature, 1936—; Spanish American literature, 1955–58; Portuguese literature, 1947–69; and Brazilian literature, 1946–69.

Twentieth Century

(B65) *Journal of Modern Literature.*
Carries an annual bibliography on Modernist writers, 1885–1950.

(B66) *Twentieth Century Literature.*
Carries a quarterly, annotated list of articles on 20th-century writers.

(D151) *Modern Drama.*
Carries an annual bibliography on 20th-century dramatists.

5. GERMAN AND NETHERLANDS LITERATURE

Although the *Bibliographie der deutschen Sprach- und Literaturwissenschaft* provides the most comprehensive coverage, both the *MLA International Bibliography* and *The Year's Work in Modern Language Studies* list items more likely to be available in North American libraries. German literary studies are included in the major period bibliographies listed in Chapter iii. Author bibliographies are listed in Chapter vi. Special subject coverage is described in Chapter v (see especially the sections on art and aesthetics, children's literature, comparative literature, film, folklore, linguistics and language, music, as well as the literary genres). General humanities periodical indexes are listed in Chapter ii.
The bibliographies here are given in order of their comprehensiveness and general availability in North American libraries.

A. GENERAL BIBLIOGRAPHIES

(A1) *MLA International Bibliography.*
International books, articles, and North American dissertations are listed in sections on general German literature, themes and types, and periods. These period sections are further subdivided for studies of bibliography, criticism, drama, poetry, prose, translations, and individual authors.

C61 *Bibliographie der deutschen Sprach- und Literaturwissenschaft.* Frankfurt am Main: Klostermann, 1957—. Annual.
The most comprehensive German bibliography. Provides classified, international coverage of books, reviews, articles, dissertations, current creative writing, and new editions of older works, 1945—. The literature part of this bibliography is arranged by period (medieval, 16th-18th cen-

turies, *Goethezeit, Romantik*, 1830–80, 1880–1914, 1914–45, and 1945—), with additional sections on literary history and theory. Each section has appropriate subdivisions, including ones for individual authors. Critic and author index, subject index (examples: *Amerika, Melancholie, Metaphor, Politik,* and *Strukturalismus*).

C62 *Germanistik: International Referatenorgan mit Bibliographischer Hinweisen.* Tübingen: Niemeyer, 1960—. 4/yr.

International, comprehensive, and classified bibliography of books, articles, and dissertations, with annotations in German. The sections: collections and general works, language and linguistics, general literary studies, literary studies by period, folk literature, and theater. Annual author and critic index and a list of editions in progress or newly published.

(C3) *The Year's Work in Modern Language Studies.*

The bibliographic essay on German literature has sections on medieval, 16th- and 17th-century, classical, Romantic, mid-19th-century, and modern literature. Author and critic index.

C63 *Beiträge zur Literaturkunde: Bibliographie ausgewählter Zeitungs- und Zeitschriftenbeiträge.** Leipzig: Bibliographisches Institut, 1952—. 2/yr.

(Vol. 1 published as Beiheft 3 of *Der Bibliothekar: Zeitschrift für das Bibliothekswessen.* Berlin: Volk und Wissen, 1946—.)

A classified, international bibliography, for 1945—, of East German (and German language socialist) books, reviews, and articles on world literature.

C64 *Referatendienst zur Germanistischen Literaturwissenschaft: Literaturwissenschaftliche Information und Dokumentation.* Berlin: Akademie der Wissenschaften der DDR, 1969—. 4/yr.

A selective, classified collection of book reviews and abstracts of articles, with emphasis on East German and German socialist publications.

C65 *JEGP: Journal of English and Germanic Philology.* Urbana: Univ. of Illinois, 1897—. 4/yr.

"Anglo-German Literary Bibliography," 1933–69, in Vols. 34–69, 1935–70, listed international books and articles.

C66 *Maske und Kothurn: Vierteljahrsschrift für Theaterwissenschaft.* Weimar: Böhlaus, 1955—. 4/yr.

Carries an annual bibliography of German books and articles on international theater, but with emphasis on German theater and German productions of non-German drama.

B. LITERARY PERIODS

Studies on literary periods are covered in the general bibliographies just listed and in the major period bibliographies listed in Chapter iii. See these in particular:

Medieval
(B15) *International Medieval Bibliography.*

Renaissance
(B30) *Bibliographie International d'Humanisme et de la Renaissance.*

C67 *Wolfenbütteler Barock-Nachrichten.* Hamburg: Hauswedell, 1974—.
4/yr.
Carries a triquarterly, international, classified, and comprehensive
bibliography of books, reviews, articles, and German dissertations on
German baroque culture. Subdivided for texts and general studies, individual authors, and book reviews.

Eighteenth Century
(B41) *The Eighteenth Century: A Current Bibliography.*
Coverage of German literature began with the 1970 bibliography.
C68 *Internationale Bibliographie zur deutschen Klassik, 1750–1850.* Wei-
mar: National Forschung- und Gedenkstätten der klassischen deutschen
Literatur in Weimar, 1964—. 2/yr.
An international classified bibliography of books, reviews, and arti-
cles. Covers cultural background, aesthetic and literary theory, and in-
dividual authors. Occasional annotations; critic and subject index.

Romanticism
(B51) *The Romantic Movement: A Selective and Critical Bibliography.*

Twentieth Century
(B65) *Journal of Modern Literature.*
Carries an annual bibliography on Modernist writers, 1885–1950.
(B66) *Twentieth Century Literature.*
Carries a quarterly, annotated list of articles on 20th-century writers.
(D151) *Modern Drama.*
Carries an annual bibliography on 20th-century dramatists.

C. NETHERLANDS LITERATURE

See coverage in the *MLA International Bibliography* (A1), *The Year's Work in
Modern Language Studies* (C3), period bibliographies, and relevant subject bibliographies (Ch. v).

C71 *Dutch Studies: An Annual Review of the Language, Literature and Life
of the Low Countries.* The Hague: Nijhoff, 1974—. Annual.
"Publications on Dutch Language and Literature in Languages Other
than Dutch" covers international books and articles on individual authors and Dutch language and literature in general.

C72 *Bibliographie van de Nederlandse Taal- en Literatuurwetenschap.*
Antwerp: Archief en Museum voor het Vlaamse Culturleven, 1970—.
Annual.
An international, classified bibliography of books and articles on
Dutch language and literature. Subject and critic indexes.

C73 *Nijhoff's Index op Nederlandse en Vlaamse Periodiken.* The Hague:
Nijhoff, 1910–71. 12/yr.
A subject index to Netherlands periodicals in all fields. Creative writ-
ing indexed by author.

6.   SCANDINAVIAN AND OLD NORSE LITERATURE

Scholarship in the Scandinavian literatures is covered in the *MLA International Bibliography* (A1) and *The Year's Work in Modern Language Studies* (C3), in *Scandinavian Studies* (C75), and in national literary yearbooks. Specialized subject bibliographies are listed in Chapter v (see especially children's literature, film, folklore, linguistics and language, and the literary genres). General literary bibliographies and humanities periodical indexes are listed in Chapter ii. Author bibliographies are in chapter vi.

A.   SCANDINAVIAN LITERATURE

(A1)   *MLA International Bibliography.*

Coverage of studies on Scandinavian literature is divided into sections on general literature, literature before 1500, and Danish, Icelandic, Norwegian, and Swedish literatures. Each national section is further subdivided for subjects and individual authors. Finnish literature is covered in the *MLA International Bibliography*, Vol. II, East European Literatures, Non-Indo-European.

(C3)   *The Year's Work in Modern Language Studies.*

Separate chapters are devoted to Danish, Norwegian, and Swedish literatures.

C75   *Scandinavian Studies.* Lawrence, Kan.: Allen, 1911—. 4/yr. (Publisher and place have varied.)

"American Scandinavian Bibliography," 1947–72 (Vol. 20–45, 1948–73) and "Scandinavia in English: A Bibliography of Books, Articles, and Book Reviews," Vol. 47, No. 4, 1975, covered studies in the social sciences and humanities. Relevant subject categories: folklore and mythology, language, literature (subdivided by nation and including film and philosophy), theater and drama, and children's books.

C76   *Acta Philologica Scandinavica/Tidsskrift for Nordisk Sprogforskning/ Journal of Scandinavian Philology.* Copenhagen: Munksgaard, 1926—. 2/yr.

"Bibliography of Scandinavian Philology," 1925—, is a classified, annotated bibliography mainly of Scandinavian books, articles, and dissertations on Scandinavian names, language, and philological aspects of literary texts. Supplemented since Vol. 29, 1970, by "Bulletin of Scandinavian Philology," a list of current books and articles, without summary annotations. The bibliography is considerably behind schedule.

C77   *Samlaren: Tidskrift för Svensk Litteraturvetenskaplig Forskning.* Uppsala: Svenska Litteratursällskapet, 1880—. Annual.

"Svensk Litteraturhistorisk Bibliografi," 1880—, is a classified bibliography mainly of Swedish books and articles on Swedish literature, including religious and folk literatures, with brief descriptive annotations in Swedish. Published separately, 1881–1928.

(B65)   *Journal of Modern Literature.*

Carries an annual bibliography of books and articles on Modernist literature, 1885–1950.

(B66)   *Twentieth Century Literature.*

Carries a quarterly, annotated bibliography of articles on 20th-century literature

(D151) *Modern Drama.*
Carries an annual bibliography of books and articles on 20th-century dramatists.

C78 *Norsk Litteraer Årbok.* Oslo: Det Norske Samlaget, 1966—. Annual.
"Bibliografi til Norsk Litteraturforsking," for 1965—, is a classified list mainly of Norwegian books and articles on Norwegian literature. Some entries are annotated in Norwegian.

C79 *Svenska Tidskriftsartiklar.* Lund: Bibliotekstjänst, 1953—. Annual.
A classified index to about 400 Swedish periodicals covering all subjects. Author index.

C80 *Dansk Tidsskrift-Index.* Copenhagen: Bibliotekscentralens, 1916—. Annual.
A classified bibliography, for 1885—, of articles in about 360 Danish periodicals on all subjects; author and subject indexes.

C81 *Norsk Tidsskriftindex.* Oslo: Steenske, 1918—. Annual.
A classified bibliography of articles in about 250 Norwegian periodicals on all subjects.

B. OLD NORSE LITERATURE

C82 *Bibliography of Old Norse and Icelandic Studies.* Copenhagen: The Royal Library, 1964—. Annual.
An international bibliography of books, reviews, and articles, 1963—, on medieval Icelandic and Norwegian language, literature, and culture. Items listed by author, or title if anonymous, with subject index. Coverage also provided in:

(A1) *MLA International Bibliography.*

(C3) *The Year's Work in Modern Language Studies.*

(C62) *Germanistik.*

7. MODERN GREEK LITERATURE

(A1) *MLA International Bibliography.*
Studies on modern Greek have been listed, 1968—.

C85 *Bibliographia Neoellénikés Philologias.* Athens: Univ. of Athens, 1959—. Annual
(Titled *Bibliographikon Deltion Neoellénikés Philologias*, 1959–65.)
An international, classified bibliography of books, reviews, and articles on modern Greek literature, philology, and culture. Critic index.

C86 *Bulletin Analytique de Bibliographie Hellénique.* Athens: Institut Français d'Athènes, 1947—. Annual.
An international, comprehensive, and classified bibliography, with abstracts, of books and articles on all aspects of modern Greece, including literature, language, and the arts. Critic and author index.

C87 *Bibliographical Bulletin of the Greek Language/Deltio Vivliographias tēs Hellēnikēs glōssēs.* Athens: Univ. of Athens, 1974—. Annual.
An international, classified bibliography, for 1973—, of books, reviews, and articles on ancient, Byzantine, and modern Greek language. Emphasizes linguistics more than philology. Author index.

8. ORIENTAL LITERATURE

The most comprehensive coverage of literary scholarship is provided by the *MLA International Bibliography*. Other bibliographies either limit coverage to individual literatures or include scholarship on other than literary subjects. The general periodical indexes listed in Chapter ii should provide increasingly useful coverage (A6–A27). See Chapter v for subject bibliographies. The arrangement here follows that of the MLA bibliography, and items are listed in order of their comprehensiveness and general availability in North American libraries.

A.   GENERAL BIBLIOGRAPHIES

(A1) *MLA International Bibliography.*

Coverage of the Asian literatures began in 1956; items were listed under the general section through 1968 and then given a separate section, 1969—. This section is subdivided into general Asian literature, bibliography, East and West relations, Near and Middle Eastern, Central Asian, South Asian, Southeast Asian, and East Asian literatures, with each further subdivided by country.

C90 *Bibliographia Asiatica.* Bad Wildungen: Asien Bucherei, 1953—. 4/yr.

An international, classified list of articles on all aspects of Near and East Asia. Items are arranged by region and then country. No index.

(D151) *Modern Drama.*

Carries an annual bibliography on 20th-century dramatists; includes the Near East, Israel, Far East, and South Asia.

B.   NEAR AND MIDDLE EASTERN LITERATURE

C91 *Journal of Arabic Literature.* Leiden: Brill, 1970—. Annual.

"Recent Publication," Vol. 4, 1973—, lists international books, with brief annotations.

"Annual Bibliography of Works on Arabic Literature Published in the Soviet Union" covers years 1973—.

"Bibliographie littéraire tunisienne" covers books on Tunisian literature, 1972—.

C92 *The Quarterly Index Islamicus: Current Books, Articles and Papers on Islamic Studies.* London: Mansell, 1977—. 4/yr.

A comprehensive, classified, international bibliography. Supplements the *Index Islamicus* and its five-year supplements (London: Mansell, 1958—). Covers 1906—.

C93 *The Middle East Journal.* Washington, D.C.: Middle East Inst., 1947—. 4/yr.

"Bibliography of Periodical Literature" is an international, classified list of articles on all aspects of the Middle East since the rise of Islam. Includes North Africa, Muslim Spain, and Israel. See section on language, literature, arts.

Cumulated: Peter M. Rossi and Wayne E. White, eds., *Articles on the Middle East, 1947–1971: A Cumulation of the Bibliographies from The Middle East Journal*, 4 vols. (Ann Arbor, Mich.: Pierian, 1980).

C94 *Revue des Études Islamiques.* Paris: Geuthner, 1927—. 2/yr.

"Abstracta Islamica," an annual supplement, is an international, classified list of books, reviews, and articles. See the sections for languages, literatures, and folklore. Critic index.

C. SOUTH AND EAST ASIAN LITERATURE

General

C95 *Bibliography of Asian Studies*. Ann Arbor, Mich.: Assn. for Asian Studies, 1969—. Annual.

(Supersedes coverage in *Journal of Asian Studies*, 1959–69, *Far Eastern Quarterly*, 1941–56, and *Bulletin of Far Eastern Bibliography*, 1936–40.)

An international, classified list, for 1941—, of books and articles on all subjects, arranged first by country and then by subject (for example, literature). Critic index.

Partially cumulated: *Cumulative Bibliography of Asian Studies, 1942–1965*, 4 vols. (Boston: Hall, 1969, 1970).

C96 *Annual Review of English Books on Asia*. Salt Lake City: Brigham Young Univ. Press, 1974—. Annual.

A list of books published in North America and Great Britain and acquired by the Harold B. Lee Library at Brigham Young University. Books are listed by country and then by subject, form (for example, bibliography and directory), and author.

C97 *Quarterly Check-List of Oriental Studies*. Darien, Conn.: American Bibliographic Service, 1959–78. 4/yr.

An international, author list of books, with an annual author, translator, and editor index. Superseded *Quarterly Check-List of Oriental Art and Archeology* and *Quarterly Check-List of Oriental Religions* (both Darien, Conn.: American Bibliographic Service, 1958–59).

(B1) *Annual Bibliography of English Language and Literature*.

Covers English language writers from India and other Asian countries. Author and critic index.

(B75) *Journal of Commonwealth Literature*.

"Annual Bibliography of Commonwealth Literature," an international, classified bibliography of books and articles, 1964—, covers studies on the literature of India, Pakistan, Sri Lanka, Singapore, and Malaysia. Also lists new creative writing.

Indian Literature

C98 *Index Indo-Asiaticus*. Calcutta: Centre for Asian Documentation, 1978—. 4/yr.

Lists contents of Indian journals and of North American and European journals with articles on Indian culture.

C99 *Guide to Indian Periodical Literature*. Gurgaon: Indian Documentation Service, 1964—. 4/yr.

Author and subject index to Indian periodicals in the humanities and social sciences. Book reviews are indexed.

Chinese Literature

C100 *Chinese Literature: Essays, Articles and Reviews*. Madison: Univ. of Wisconsin, 1978—. 2/yr.

"Recent Publications on Chinese Literature," a review article, covers the current scholarship in specific countries.

C101 *Publishing and Research Semimonthly.** Taipei: Ch'eng-wen, 1977—. 24/yr.

Each issue carries a classified subject index to current articles in Taiwan periodicals and newspapers.

C102   *Bibliography Quarterly.* * Taipei: Student Book, 1966—. 4/yr.
Each issue carries an index to scholarly books and articles in literature, history, and philosophy.

C103   *China Aktuell.* Hamburg: Institut für Asiankunde, 1972—. 12/yr.
"Articles of China" is a selective, classified list of articles mainly concerned with public affairs but including five or ten items per issue on culture, literature, and the arts.

C104   *Doctoral Dissertations on Asia.* Ann Arbor: Xerox Univ. Microfilms, for the Assn. for Asian Studies, 1975–77.
Listed dissertations on all aspects of Asia, and continued coverage formerly in Frank J. Shulman, ed., *Doctoral Dissertations on China, 1971–1975: A Bibliography of Studies of Western Languages* (Seattle: Univ. of Washington Press, 1978), and Leonard H. Gordon and Frank J. Shulman, eds., *Doctoral Dissertations on China: A Bibliography of Studies in Western Languages, 1945–1970* (Seattle: Assn. for Asian Studies, 1972).

Japanese Literature

C105   *Books and Articles on Oriental Subjects Published in Japan during [year].* Tokyo: Inst. of Eastern Culture, 1957—. Annual.
A classified bibliography of books and articles. Critic index.

C106   *Zasshi Kiji Sakuin; Jinbun-Shakai-Hen.* Tokyo: National Diet Library, 1948—. 12/yr.
An index to Japanese periodicals covering the humanities and social sciences.
Cumulated for 1955–74: *Zasshi Kiji Sakuin; Jinbun-Shakai-Hen. Ruiseki Sakuin Ban* (Tokyo: National Diet Library, 1977).

C107   *Asiatic Research Bulletin.* Seoul: Asiatic Research Center, 1957—. 4/yr.
A classified list of Korean books and articles on all aspects of Korea.

9.   AFRICAN LITERATURE

There are as yet no specialized bibliographies for individual African national literatures, but there are several general bibliographies. In addition to the titles listed in this section, one should consult appropriate subject bibliographies, such as black studies and folklore (Chapter v), and the humanities periodical indexes listed in Chapter ii.

(A1)   *MLA International Bibliography.*
Coverages of black African literatures began in 1965. Starting in 1969 they were given a separate section, which is subdivided into general, bibliography, folklore, and literature, and further subdivided for the major language groups of Arabic, English, French, Portuguese, and Swahili.

(B1)   *Annual Bibliography of English Language and Literature.*
Coverage includes all writers in English. Items are arranged by century, and there is an author and critic index.

(B75) *Journal of Commonwealth Literature.*
   The "Annual Bibliography of Commonwealth Literature," 1964—,
covers Africa in general, Southern and Western African nations, and
South Africa (this last has been covered in Part II since Vol. 10, 1975).
Lists creative writing and literary studies.

C111 *A Current Bibliography on African Affairs.* Farmingdale, N.Y.:
Baywood, 1962—. 4/yr.
   A selective, classified, international bibliography of books and articles
on various aspects of African affairs. See sections for literature, linguistics, plays and drama, mass communication, and folktales.

C112 *Journal des Africanistes.* Paris: Société des Africanistes, 1931—. 2/yr.
   (Titled *Journal de la Société des Africanistes*, 1931–75.)
   Carries an annual, classified bibliography mainly of French language
books and articles on all aspects and areas of Africa. See sections on linguistics, arts, and literature.

C113 *International African Bibliography.* London: Mansell, 1971—. 4/yr.
   An international, comprehensive, classified bibliography of books and
articles, for 1971—, on several aspects of Africa, with items arranged by
broad subject area and then by region and nation. See section for language and literature. Critic index.
   Coverage supersedes that for 1928–70 in *Africa: Journal of the International African Institute* (London: Oxford Univ. Press).

C114 *Africana Journal: A Bibliographic and Review Quarterly.* New York:
Africana, 1970—. 4/yr.
   (Formerly *Africana Library Journal*, 1970–73.)
   Each issue carries a classified, international bibliography of books on
all aspects of Africa. Items arranged by subject and then by region or
country. See sections on children's literature, folklore, languages, linguistics and literature, and literary criticism. Critic and subject indexes.

C115 *African Abstracts: Quarterly Review of Articles in Current Periodicals.*
London: International African Inst., 1950—. 4/yr.
   Abstracts international articles on all aspects of Africa, including literature, language, arts, and folklore. Arranged by subject and then by region or country. Annual critic, ethnic, and linguistic indexes.

C116 *Research in African Literatures.* Austin: Univ. of Texas Press, 1970—.
3/yr.
   Current North American dissertations on African literature are listed
at least once per year.

10. EAST EUROPEAN LITERATURE

   These literatures are particularly well served by bibliographies of current
scholarship, although in North America access to both the bibliographies and the
studies is not so easy as it is for other literatures. Besides the items listed here,
one should consult appropriate subject bibliographies in Chapter v, author bibliographies in Chapter vi, and humanities periodical indexes in Chapter ii.

A. GENERAL BIBLIOGRAPHIES

   (A1) *MLA International Bibliography.*
      Limited coverage in the general studies section began in 1929. In 1950
a separate section for East European literatures was added, and the

present detailed coverage began with the 1967 bibliography. Each issue covers literature and folklore. Russian literature is a subsection under East Slavic Literature. Other headings are General and Miscellaneous, Baltic and Balto-Slavic, East Slavic (Russian, Ukrainian, Belorussian), West Slavic (Czech, Polish, Slovak), and South Slovak (Bulgarian and Yugoslavian), Non-Indo-European (Finnish, Estonian, Hungarian), Folklore, and Albanian.

(C3)   *The Year's Work in Modern Language Studies.*
Covers international studies of Czech, Slovak, Polish, Russian, Belorussian, Ukrainian, and Serbo-Croatian language and literature.

C121   *American Bibliography of Slavic and East European Studies for* [year]. Columbus, Ohio: American Assn. for Advancement of Slavic Studies, 1957—. Annual.
A classified bibliography of North American books, articles, and dissertations on all areas of Slavic and East European studies. Chapters on language and linguistics and on literature are subdivided by national language. Book reviews listed separately. Writer and critic indexes.

C122   *Soviet, East European and Slavonic Studies in Britain.* Glasgow: Univ. of Glasgow, 1971—. Annual.
A classified bibliography of books, reviews, articles, and newspaper stories published in Great Britain. Items are arranged by country and then subject, with headings under Russian literature for individual authors. Editions and translations are listed if published in Great Britain. Critic index.

C123   *Bibliographic Guide to Soviet and East European Studies.* Boston: Hall, 1978—. Annual.
An international bibliography of books, serials, and other separate publications cataloged by the Library of Congress and the New York Public Library, 1978—. Items arranged by author, title, and subject.

C124   *Slavic Review: American Quarterly of Soviet and East European Studies.* Urbana, Ill.: American Assn. for the Advancement of Slavic Studies, 1941—. 4/yr.
"Doctoral Dissertations on Russia, the Soviet Union, and Eastern Europe Accepted by American, Canadian, and British Universities," for 1960—, is an annual listing (in Vol. 23—, 1964—).

C125   *Revue Slavistique/Rocznik Slawistyczny.* Warsaw: Ossolineum, 1908—. Annual.
Carried an international, comprehensive, classified bibliography of books, reviews, and articles on all Slavic languages and literatures, 1908–72 (through Vol. 49, 1973). Editorial matter in French and Polish. Critic index. *Revue Slavistique* now regularly publishes bibliographies on a variety of subjects.

(D151)   *Modern Drama.*
Carries an annual, international bibliography of books and articles on 20th-century dramatists.

B. INDIVIDUAL COUNTRIES

U.S.S.R

C131 *Novaia Sovetskaia Literatura po Literaturovedeniiu.* Moscow: Inst. for Scholarly Information on the Social Sciences of the Academy of Sciences of the U.S.S.R., 1953—. 12/yr.

Lists Soviet books and articles on world literature.

C132 *Novaia Inostrannaia Literatura po Literaturovedeniiu.* * Moscow: Inst. for Scholarly Information in the Social Sciences of the Academy of Sciences of the U.S.S.R., 1960—. 12/yr.

Lists non-Soviet publications on world literature. Items arranged by area and subject.

C133 *Sovetskaia Khudozhestvennaia Literatura i Kritika.* Moscow: Sovetskii Pisatel, 1952—. 2/yr.

A classified bibliography of current Soviet creative writing and criticism (books, reviews, articles). Author, critic, and title index and an index to Russian language translations of other Soviet writing.

C134 *Sovetskoe Literaturovedenie i Kritika: Russkaia Sovetskaia Literatura.* Moscow: Nauka, 1966—. Irregular.

A classified bibliography of Russian language books, reviews, articles on Soviet literature. Author and subject indexes.

Poland

C135 *Literatura Piękna: Adnotowany Rocznik Bibliograficzny.* Warsaw: Stowarzyszenie Bibliotekarzy Polskich, 1956—. Annual.

A classified bibliography of Polish books, reviews, and articles on Polish literature. Abstracts. Critic and subject indexes. Translations into Polish are listed.

Yugoslavia

C136 *Bibliografska Građa.* Belgrade: Jugoslovenski Bibliografski Inst., 1968—. Annual.

A classified, international bibliography of books and articles on Yugoslavian literature. Critic and subject index.

Hungary

C137 *A Magyar Irodalom Bibliográfiája.* Budapest: Muvelt, 1950—. 5/yr.

A classified bibliography of mainly Hungarian books and articles, for 1945—, on Hungarian arts and letters, including radio, television, and film. Critic index.

C138 *Irodalomtörténeti Közlemények.* Budapest: Akadémia Kiadó, 1891—. 4/yr.

Carries an annual list of books and articles, 1962—, on Hungarian literary history.

Chapter Five.   Subjects

Chapters ii, iii, and iv list literary bibliographies for national literatures and literary periods; this chapter includes bibliographies for literary genres, themes and concerns, specialized research and reference materials, subjects fairly closely related to literature (such as art and aesthetics, history, and popular culture), other broad subject areas, language and linguistics—anything, in short, that would be needed by, or of use to, literary scholars and teachers. Although English, American, and Commonwealth literature subjects and sources are emphasized, students working in other languages can find many useful bibliographies here. In most of the subject categories the list of bibliographies is selective, not exhaustive. Those bibliographies included are either comprehensive or accessible to North American scholars and are especially relevant to literary research or to researchers with historical, philosophical, or humanistic interests.

The categories are listed alphabetically, with some cross-references. The detailed table of contents lists the categories; the index gives a detailed subject breakdown.

AFRICAN STUDIES. See Chapter iv, Section 9.

AMERICAN STUDIES
    At present there is no regular, comprehensive bibliography of American studies; therefore, the researcher must consult the more specialized bibliographies in various areas of American studies. See also sections on folklore, history, humor, journalism and mass communication, linguistics and language, popular culture, regionalism, and women's studies, as well as the American literature section in Chapter iii.

   D1 *American Quarterly.* Philadelphia: Univ. of Pennsylvania, 1949—. 4/yr.
        "American Studies Research in Progress," Vol. 27—, 1975—, is an annual checklist of dissertations and other projects in progress or completed. Dissertations were previously listed under "American Studies Dissertations," Vols. 8–26, 1956–74.
        "Articles in American Studies," for 1954–72 (Vols. 7–25, 1955–73), was an annual, selective, classified bibliography of articles dealing with a relationship between two or more aspects of American culture (and which had not been published in *American Quarterly*). Replaced by a bibliography issue that carries enumerative and review bibliographies on a variety of subjects.

Partially cumulated: Henig Cohen, *Articles in American Studies,
1954–68: A Cumulation of the Annual Bibliographies from* American
Quarterly, 2 vols. (Ann Arbor: Pierian, 1972).

D2 *Amerikastudien/American Studies.* Stuttgart: Metzlersche, 1956—.
2/yr.

(Formerly *Jahrbuch für Amerikastudien*, Vols. 1–18, 1956–73.)
"Deutsche amerikanistische Veröffentlichungen," for 1945—, is an
annual classified bibliography of German books and articles on American
studies. Items are listed by author under several broad subject areas,
such as *Sprache und Literatur.*

D3 *German Quarterly.* Cherry Hill, N.J.: American Assn. of Teachers of
German, 1928—. 4/yr. (Place has varied.)
"Bibliography Americana Germanica," 1967–69 (Vols. 41–43, 1968–
70), was an annual bibliography of books, articles, and dissertations on
German-American literary, historical, cultural relations. Coverage was
previously carried for 1941–66 in *American German Review* (Philadelphia: National Carl Schurz Foundation).

(A1) *MLA International Bibliography.*
"Americana Germanica" has been a subsection under German literature, 1926—. Title has varied.

(C65) *JEGP: Journal of English and Germanic Philology.*
See "Anglo-German Literary Bibliography."

(C32) *Italica.*
Lists Italian-American studies for 1975— (in Vol. 52—). Such studies
were previously listed in the general section of the bibliography.

(D350) *Journal of American Culture.*
See the regular checklist, "Technology in American Culture: Recent
Publications," for 1980—.

ART, AESTHETICS, ARCHITECTURE

See also bibliographies listed under comparative literature, critical and literary
theory, and philosophy.

D6 *Art Index.* New York: Wilson, 1929—. 4/yr., with annual cumulation.
An author and subject index to American and European periodicals
dealing with art and aesthetics. Subjects covered include broad areas
such as art, architecture, art history, city planning, film, arts and crafts,
interior and landscape design, and specific subjects such as art and literature, aesthetics, criticism, Romanticism, concrete poetry, and exhibits
of artists' and writers' work.

D7 *RILA. Répertoire Internationale de la Littérature de l'Art/Inter-
national Repertory of the Literature of Art.* Williamstown, Mass.: College Art Assn. 1975—. 2/yr.
A classified, international list, with abstracts, of books, reviews, articles, newspaper stories, festschriften, proceedings, exhibition catalogs,
museum publications, and dissertations in the fields of post-Classical
European and post-Columbian American art. Author and subject index
in each issue.

D8 *Répertoire d'Art et d'Archéologie.* Paris: Centre National de la Recherche Scientifique, 1910—. 5/yr.

An international, classified bibliography, with brief annotations, of articles on archaeology, sculpture, painting, and arts. Artist, critic, and subject index in each issue, cumulated in the fifth issue.

D9   *Bulletin Signalétique 526: Art et Archéologie; Proche-Orient, Asie, Amérique,* Paris: Centre National de la Recherche Scientifique, 1948—. 12/yr.

An international, classified, annotated bibliography of articles on various aspects of art and archaeology, for 1947—. A monthly author and subject index is cumulated annually.

(A1) *MLA International Bibliography.*

See Vol. I under General Literature and Related Topics. I. Esthetics.

D10 *Journal of Aesthetics and Art Criticism.* Philadelphia: American Soc. for Aesthetics, 1941—. 4/yr.

"Selective Current Bibliography for Aesthetics and Related Fields," for 1941–72 (Vols. 1–31, 1941–73), was an annual, international bibliography of books and articles on the philosophy and psychology of art.

(D307) *Bibliographie de la Philosophie/Bibliography of Philosophy.*

Lists new books on aesthetics and the philosophy of art.

(D308) *Répertoire Bibliographique de la Philosophie.*

Lists international books and articles on art and aesthetics.

D11 *Bibliographie zur Symbolik, Ikonographie und Mythologie.* Baden-Baden: Koerner, 1968—. Annual.

An international, comprehensive author list of books and articles, with annotations in French, German, or English. Subject index.

D12 *Dada/Surrealism.** New York: Queens College Press, 1971—. Annual.

See "A Selected Bibliography of Works on Dada/Surrealism Published in North America."

ARTHURIAN STUDIES

D15 *Bulletin Bibliographique de la Société Internationale Arthurienne/ Bibliographical Bulletin of the International Arthurian Society.* Paris: Société Internationale Arthurienne, 1948—. Annual.

An international, comprehensive, classified, annotated bibliography of books and articles on Arthurian matters. Items are arranged by country and then for major subjects, if there are sufficient entries. Annotations are in the language of the item. Author and critic index; subject and title index.

(A1) *MLA International Bibliography.*

See Vol. I under General Literature and Related Topics. IV. Themes and Types.

D16 *Modern Language Quarterly.* Seattle: Univ. of Washington, 1940—. 4/yr.

"A Bibliography of Critical Arthurian Literature," for 1936–62 (Vols. 1–24, 1940–63), provided international, comprehensive coverage of books, reviews, and articles, with occasional brief annotations.

Scholarship for 1922–35 was covered in *A Bibliography of Critical Arthurian Literature.* (New York: Modern Language Assn., 1931 and 1936).

ASIAN STUDIES. See Chapter iv, Section 8.

BIBLIOGRAPHY: ENUMERATIVE: AUTHORS AND SUBJECTS.
For analytical bibliography, see the next section.

D19 *Bibliographic Index: A Cumulative Bibliography of Bibliographies.*
New York: Wilson, 1937—. 3/yr., including annual cumulation.
A subject index to bibliographies consisting of 50 or more items published separately or as parts of books or articles. About 2,400 international periodicals (but predominantly in English, Germanic, or Romance languages) are scanned regularly.

D20 *Bibliographische Berichte/Bibliographical Bulletin.* Frankfurt am Main: Klosterman, 1949—. 2/yr., with annual cumulation.
(Supersedes *Bibliographische Beihefte zur Zeitschrift für Bibliothekswesen und Bibliographie*, 1957–58.)
Complements *Bibliographic Index*, especially in East European coverage. A classified list of bibliographies published separately or in books or articles. See, for example, *Philologie*/Language and Literature, under which are such subheadings as *Anglistik, Germanistik, Skandinavistik.*

(B1) *Annual Bibliography of English Language and Literature.*
A general bibliography section includes bibliographies on themes, subjects, and genres.

BIBLIOGRAPHY: ANALYTICAL: TEXTUAL STUDIES
See also the sections on book trade, libraries, journalism and mass communication, and periodicals.

D23 *ABHB. Annual Bibliography of the History of the Printed Book and Libraries.* The Hague: Nijhoff, 1973—. Annual.
An international, classified bibliography of books, reviews, and articles, for 1970—. Chapters list items about the history of books and libraries, printing materials, calligraphy and type, printing, book illustration, bookbinding, publishing and the book trade, collecting, institutions and libraries, the legal, economic, and social aspects of books and libraries, newspapers and journalism, and related subjects. Name index provides access to studies on specific writers.

D24 *Studies in Bibliography.* Charlottesville: Bibliographical Soc. of Virginia, 1948—. Annual.
"A Selective Checklist of Bibliographical Scholarship," for 1949–71 (Vols. 3–26, 1950–73), listed international books and articles dealing with incunabula, early printing, bibliographies, check lists and enumeration, printing and publishing, and bibliography and textual scholarship,
Cumulated: Rudolf Hirsch and Howell Haney, *Selective Check Lists of Bibliographical Scholarship. 1949–1955. Studies in Bibliography*, Vol. 10. (Charlottesville: Univ. of Virginia, 1957), and *Selective Check Lists of Bibliographical Scholarship, Series B, 1956–1962* (Charlottesville: Univ. Press of Virginia, 1966).

D25 *Index to Reviews of Bibliographical Publications.* Boston: Hall, 1978—. Annual.
An annual author index to North American reviews, 1977—, of international bibliographical publications, including editions of literary

texts and materials (such as letters and manuscripts) and books about textual matters. Also serves as a checklist of current bibliographical publications. The bibliography for 1976 was carried in *Analytical and Enumerative Bibliography* (DeKalb: Bibliographical Soc. of Northern Illinois), 1 (1977), 273–437.

(A1)   *MLA International Bibliography.*

International books and articles about books, collections, bibliographical theory, and textual studies are listed under General Literature and Related Topics. V. Bibliographical.

(B1)   *Annual Bibliography of English Language and Literature.*

The general bibliography section cites studies on textual bibliography and related subjects pertaining to English language literature.

D26   *The Library: The Transactions of the Bibliographical Society.* London: Bibliographical Soc., 1899—. 4/yr.

Each issue, Vol. 20, 1965—, has two sections of note: "Recent Books" lists, with brief summaries, recent studies in analytical and descriptive bibliography, and "Recent Periodicals" selectively lists the contents of North American and European literary, historical, and bibliographical journals.

D27   *Proof: The Yearbook of American Bibliographical and Textual Studies.* Columbia, S.C.: Faust, 1971–77. Annual.

"The Register of Current Publications" listed books, monographs, and pamphlets of interest to textual critics. Covered editions, subject and author checklists, national bibliographies, and studies, and listed scholarly tools on literature, writing, printing, publishing, bookselling, libraries and collecting, and bibliographic theory and practice.

D28   *The Direction Line: A Newsletter for Bibliographers and Textual Critics.* Austin: Univ. of Texas, 1975—. 2/yr.

Carries a regular bibliographic essay on textual matters, "A Review of the Year's Research."

(D50)   *Annual Report of the American Rare, Antiquarian and Out-of-Print Book Trade.*

Carries an annual review article, "Trends in Bibliography."

BIOGRAPHY

The items listed here either provide information about literary figures or lead to studies of biography as a genre. None of the many directories of people in professions, organizations, and activities is listed.

D30   *Biography Index: A Cumulative Index to Biographical Material in Books and Magazines.* New York: Wilson, 1946—. 4/yr.

A name index to biographical information on people living or dead published in international books and articles. Presence of portraits is noted. An index to professions and occupations lists names under such headings as painters, parachutists, peasants, and poets.

D31   *Contemporary Authors: A Bio-Bibliographical Guide to Current Writers in Fiction, General Nonfiction, Poetry, Journalism, Drama, Motion Pictures, Television, and Other Fields.* Detroit: Gale, 1962—. Annual.

Provides up-to-date information on living authors, chiefly American, in all subjects and all kinds of writing. Entries include biographies, brief bibliographies, and, often, comment by the authors about their writing. Most volumes include a cumulative index, and earlier volumes are revised to accommodate new information.

(A1) *MLA International Bibliography.*
Studies of biography as a genre are listed in Vol. I under General Literature and Related Topics. IV. Themes and Types, and under the various literary period subsections of English and American literature.

(B1) *Annual Bibliography of English Language and Literature.*
See the section Biography for studies of biography as a genre.

(B6) *English Studies.*
See the annual review article, "Current Literature II: Criticism and Biography."

D32 *Current Biography.* New York: Wilson, 1940—. 12/yr., with annual cumulation.
Provides biographical articles on newsworthy people from all countries. Annual index, with ten-year cumulations.

BLACK STUDIES
See also under Regionalism (U.S.A.), below.

D37 *CLA Journal: A Quarterly.* Baltimore: College Language Assn., 1957—. 4/yr.
"An Annual Bibliography of Afro-American Litarature, [year], with Selected Bibliographies of African and Caribbean Literature," 1975–76 (Vols. 20–21, 1976–77) listed creative writing and scholarly books and articles. Each of three parts (Afro-American, African, Caribbean) is subdivided into sections on anthologies and collections, autobiography and biography, bibliography, drama, fiction, folklore, poetry, general literary criticism and history, and miscellaneous. The five genre sections list individual works, general criticism, and criticism on individual authors.

D38 *Obsidian: Black Literature in Review.* Fredonia: State Univ. of New York, College at Fredonia, 1975—. 3/yr.
"Studies in Afro-American Literature: An Annual Annotated Bibliography," 1974–76, was comparable to the listing in the *CLA Journal* but with the addition of annotations.

(A1) *MLA International Bibliography.*
Studies on Afro-American literature in general are listed under "Afro-American" in all five sections of American Literature in Vol. I.

D39 *Index to Periodical Articles by and about Blacks.* Boston: Hall, 1950—. Annual.
An author and subject index to about 50 black American periodicals. Covers creative writing, literary studies, and Afro-American life in general.

D40 *Bibliographic Guide to Black Studies.* Boston: Hall, 1976—. Annual.
An author, subject, and title list of international books and monographs cataloged by the Library of Congress and the New York Public Library, for 1975—.
Updates: *Dictionary Catalog of the Schomburg Collection of Negro Literature and History*, 9 vols. (Boston: Hall, 1962; first supplement, 2 vols., 1967; second supplement, 4 vols., 1972).

BOOK REVIEWS

Only book review indexes are listed here, not book-reviewing journals such as the *New York Times Book Review* and the *Times Literary Supplement*. See also the general periodical indexes (A6–A26) and various period, author, and subject bibliographies.

D45   *Current Book Review Citations.* New York: Wilson, 1976—. 11/yr., with annual cumulation.

An author and title index to book reviews in about 1,200 North American and British periodicals and three newspapers, for books on all subjects, including creative writing, and from all countries.

D46   *Book Review Index.* Detroit: Gale, 1965—. 6/yr., with annual cumulation.

An author, title index to reviews in about 330 predominantly North American periodicals. Reviews cover creative writing and scholarly studies. Title index was added with Vol. 12, 1976.

(B1) *Annual Bibliography of English Language and Literature.*
Cites reviews of the books it lists.

D47   *Index to Book Reviews in the Humanities.* Williamstown, Mich.: Phillip Thompson, 1960—. Annual.

An author index to book reviews in humanities and related social sciences published in about 360 international journals.

D48   *Internationale Bibliographie der Rezensionen wissenschaftlicher Literatur/International Review of Book Reviews of Scholarly Literature.* Osnabrück: Dietrich, 1971—. 6/yr.

Indexes book reviews from about 1,000 international journals in all fields in three ways: subject classified list of books reviewed, author list of books reviewed, and reviewer list. Entries provide cross references (for example, under Abélard, see also Héloïse) and explanatory notes about subjects (for example, *Kommunication* [biol.]). Continues Part C of the *International Bibliographie der Zeitschriftenliteratur* (A11), 1901–44.

D49   *Book Review Digest.* New York: Wilson, 1905—. 12/yr., with annual cumulation.

An author, title, and subject index to book reviews in about 90 North American general interest periodicals. Excerpts of some reviews are provided. To be included, a book must have been published or distributed in the U.S.A., must have had two reviews if nonfiction and four if fiction, and its reviews must have appeared within 18 months of its publication.

(D268) *The American Book Review.*
(B85) *Canadian Book Review Annual.*
(B78) *Index to Australian Book Reviews.*

BOOK TRADE

The bibliographies here tend to cover the historical aspects of the book trade; for more current topics see *Library Literature* (D245), *Library and Information Science Abstracts* (D246), and the *Business Periodicals Index* (D160). See also the major bibliographies for national literatures and literary periods and for little magazines and small presses.

(D23) *ABHB. Annual Bibliography of the History of the Printed Book and Libraries.*
Covers studies of the book trade and publishing, paper, printing and binding, and book collecting.

(A1) *MLA International Bibliography.*
The book trade, publishing (especially that of the small presses), and bookselling are included in Vol. I under General Literature and Related Topics. V. Bibliographical. See also under Bibliography for national literatures and for specific literary periods.

(B1) *Annual Bibliography of English Language and Literature.*
See Book Production, Selling, Collecting, in Vol. 25—, 1934—. With Vol. 48, 1973, the coverage has been expanded.

D50 *Annual Report of the American Rare, Antiquarian and Out-of-Print Book Trade.* New York: BCAR, 1979—. Annual.
Part VI, "Trends in Bibliography," has review articles discussing work on major American bibliographic tools, on trends in codicology, analytical and historical bibliography, and on analytical bibliography and literature.

CARIBBEAN STUDIES. See Chapter iv, Nos. C48-C55.

CELTIC STUDIES
See also the separate sections for history, Irish literature, Scottish studies, and Arthurian studies.

(A1) *MLA International Bibliography.*
Celtic Literatures, with subsections on Breton, Cornish, Irish Gaelic, Manx, Scottish Gaelic, and Welsh subjects, is a major section in Vol. I.

(C3) *The Year's Work in Modern Language Studies.*
Annual coverage of Breton, Cornish, Irish, Gaelic, Manx, Scottish Gaelic, and Welsh literatures, 1930–36, 1974—.

D55 *Bibliotheca Celtica: A Register of Publications Relating to Wales and the Celtic Peoples and Languages.* Aberystwyth: National Library of Wales, 1910—. Irregular.
Comprehensive, international, classified bibliography of books, articles, and pamphlets on all aspects of current and historic Celtic life. Author and subject index.

D56 *Études Celtiques.* Paris: Société d'Edition "Les Belles Lettres," 1936—. Annual.
"Periodiques" is an author list with abstracts of French articles on Celtic studies.

CHILDREN'S LITERATURE
See also bibliographies for nineteenth- and twentieth-century English and American literature and for folklore, popular culture, education, and libraries.

(A1) *MLA International Bibliography.*
Studies in children's literature, for 1976—, are listed in a subsection under General Literature and Related Topics. IV. Themes and Types.

(B1) *Annual Bibliography of English Language and Literature.*
Starting with Vol. 50 for 1975 (1978), Literature for Children is a subsection under English Literature. General.

D60 *Phaedrus: An International Journal of Children's Literature Research.* New York: Sauer, 1973—. 2/yr.
Each issue carries an international list of books, articles, dissertations, catalogs, and bibliographies.

D61 *Children's Literature Review. Excerpts from Reviews, Criticism, and Commentary on Books for Children and Young People.* Gale: Detroit, 1976—. Annual.
Excerpts current critical comment in books, reviews, and articles on writers and their works. British and American writers are emphasized, but non-English writers are selectively included. Author, title, and critic indexes.

D62 *Children's Literature Abstracts.* Birmingham: International Federation of Library Assns., 1973—. 4/yr.
An international, comprehensive, and classified bibliography of articles on children's literature, with brief descriptive summaries in English. Annual critic and subject index.

CLASSICAL LITERATURE

D70 *L'Année Philologique: Bibliographie Critique et Analytique de l'Antiquité Greco-Latine.* Paris: Société d'Edition "Les Belles Lettres." 1924—. Annual.
An annual, international, comprehensive, classified bibliography of books and articles. Part I lists studies of individual authors and texts; Part II lists, in classified form, studies on literature, language, archaeology, history, law, science, and classical studies. There are indexes for collective titles listed in Part I (such as *Anthologia Graeca*), for classical names, for Renaissance and later humanists, and for critics.
Coverage continues: *Dix Années de Bibliographie Classique: Bibliographie Critique et Analytique de l'Antiquité Greco-Latine pour la Periode 1914–1924*, 2 vols (Paris: Société d'Edition "Les Belles Lettres," 1927, 1928), and *Bibliographie de l'Antiquité Classique 1896–1914*. Part I. (Paris: Société d'Edition "Les Belles Lettres," 1951).

D71 *Gnomon: Kritische Zeitschrift für die Gesamte Klassische Altertumswissenschaft.* Munich: Beck'sche, 1925—. 8/yr.
"Bibliographische Beilage" in every other issue is a comprehensive, international, classified list of books and articles on history, literature, and other aspects of classical culture.

D72 *International Guide to Classical Studies: A Continuous Guide to Periodical Literature.* Darien, Conn.: American Bibliographic Service, 1961–78. 4/yr.
An international and comprehensive author list, for 1960–73, of articles, with annual cumulative author and subject index.

D73 *Quarterly Check-List of Classical Studies: An International Index of Current Books, Monographs, Brochures, and Separates.* Darien, Conn.: American Bibliographic Service, 1958–78. 4/yr.
An international and comprehensive author list, for 1958–77, of books on all aspects of the classical world. Annual author, editor, and translator index.

D74 *American Classical Review.* New York: City Univ. of New York, 1971—. 4/yr.

"Doctoral Dissertations in Progress" is an annual list by institution of American and Canadian dissertations in classical studies.

COMMUNICATION
See Journalism and Mass Communication and Speech Communication.

COMPARATIVE LITERATURE AND TRANSLATION

A. Comparative Literature
Because comparative literature studies deal not only with relationships between two or more literatures but also with relationships between literature and other arts and subjects, anyone searching for comparative studies should look into relevant bibliographies listed in other sections of this chapter (such as art and aesthetics, music, psychology, science, and theology) as well as those listed in Chapter iv on the non-English literatures.

(A1) *MLA International Bibliography.*
See Vol. I under General Literature and Related Topics. III. Literature, General and Comparative.

D80 *Canadian Review of Comparative Literature/Revue Canadienne de Littérature Comparée.* Toronto: Univ. of Toronto Press, 1974—. 4/yr.

"Revue des Revues" is an annual, annotated, international, and classified list of articles on comparative literature, for 1973—. Has sections for studies of literary history and relationships, literary theory and critical methodology, and literature in the other arts.

"Preliminary Bibliography of Comparative Canadian Literature (English-Canadian and French-Canadian)," 1976—, is an annual classified list of books, articles, and dissertations. The first bibliography was retrospective; subsequent ones cover each year's work in the field.

(B1) *Annual Bibliography of English Language and Literature.*
See coverage in Vols. 4–35, 1923–60.

D81 *A Bibliography on the Relations of Literature and the Other Arts.* Hanover, N.H.: Dartmouth College, 1978—. Annual.

An international, comprehensive bibliography of books and articles on the relations between literature and music, art, and film, and on the theory of comparative studies. Compiled and issued annually by the MLA Division on Literature and the Other Arts (formerly General Topics IX), 1952—.

Years 1973–75 were carried in Vols. 6–8 of *Hartford Studies in Literature* (Hartford, Conn.: Univ. of Hartford, 1974–76). Years 1952–67 have been collected: *A Bibliography on the Relations of Literature and the Other Arts 1952–67* (New York, AMS, 1968). This volume includes: *Literature and the Other Arts: A Select Bibliography 1952–1958* (New York: New York Public Library, 1959).

D82 *Comparative Criticism: A Yearbook.* Cambridge: Cambridge Univ. Press, 1979—. Annual.

"Bibliography of Comparative Literature in Britain," for 1975—, is a classified list of books and articles published in Britain or by British scholars. Arrangement follows that in the *Yearbook of Comparative and General Literature* (D83).

D83 *Yearbook of Comparative and General Literature.* Bloomington: Indiana Univ., 1952—. Annual.

(Vols. 1–9, 1952–60, were published at Chapel Hill as the *University of North Carolina Studies in Comparative Literature*.)

An international and comprehensive bibliography of comparative literature studies, for 1949–69 (in Vols. 1–20, 1952–70), listed books, articles, and dissertations on themes and genres, on literary influences and relationships, on individual authors and countries, and (in some years) on relations between literature and other arts and between literature and science.

Updates Fernand Baldensperger and Werner F. Friederich, *Bibliography of Comparative Literature* (Chapel Hill: Univ. of North Carolina, 1950).

D84 *Revue de Littérature Comparée.* Paris: Didier, 1921—. 4/yr.

Carried a bibliography of international comparative literature studies in each quarterly issue, Vols. 1–34, 1921–60.

Those for 1949–58 were reprinted: *Bibliographie Generale de Littérature Comparée* (Paris: Boivin, 1951–59).

(C65) *JEGP: Journal of English and Germanic Philology.*

"Anglo-German Literary Bibliography," 1933–69, listed books and articles on Anglo-German literary relations.

B. Translation

(A1) *MLA International Bibliography.*

Studies on the art and practice of translation are listed in Vol. I under General Literature and Related Topics. IV. Themes and Types.

D90 *Index Translationum.* Paris: UNESCO, 1932—. Annual. (Suspended 1941–47.)

An annual, classified bibliography of translations of books in all subjects and into all languages. Arranged by country and then according to the Universal Decimal Scheme. Author index.

D91 *Translation Review.** Dallas: Univ. of Texas at Dallas, Center for Writing and Translation, 1976—. 6/yr.

Regularly reviews all books translated into English and lists translations in progress.

D92 *Babel: Revue Internationale de Traduction.* Gerlingen: Federation Internationale des Traductions, 1955—. 4/yr.

Carries an international, biannual bibliography of books and articles on translation (excluding works published in FIT organs).

(D83) *Yearbook of Comparative and General Literature.*

Lists translations of literary works, Vol. 10, 1961—.

D93 *Chartotheca Translationum Alphabetica/International Bibliography of Translations.* Bad Homburg: Bentz, 1962—.

An author list of international translations for 1961—. Coverage is complex; see the bibliography's introduction for an explanation.

COMPOSITION AND RHETORIC

D95 *College Composition and Communication: The Journal of the Conference on College Composition and Communication.* Urbana, Ill.: National Council of Teachers of English, 1950—. 4/yr.

An annual, selective and annotated bibliography of books and articles on composition, 1973— (Vol. 26, 1975—), includes only studies that report original and significant research or that record new or noteworthy ideas about the philosophy and teaching of composition.

D96   *Research in the Teaching of English.* Urbana, Ill.: National Council of Teachers of English, 1967—. 4/yr.

"Annotated Bibliography of Research in the Teaching of English," for 1966—, is a biannual, classified bibliography of books, articles, dissertations, and papers.

D97   *Technical Communication: Journal of the Society for Technical Communication.* Washington, D.C.: Soc. for Technical Communication, 1953—. 4/yr.

A "Recent and Relevant" section, in each issue starting with 1976, lists abstracts of articles from about fifty journals.

D98   *Technical Writing Teacher.* Morehead, Ky.: Assn. of Teachers of Technical Writing, 1974—. 2/yr.

Carries an annual, international, and selective list of books and articles on various aspects of technical writing.

D99   *Rhetorik: Ein Internationales Jahrbuch.* Stuttgart: Frommann-Holzboog, 1980—. Annual.

Carries a continuing bibliography of international rhetoric research.

D100 *Rhetoric Society Quarterly.** St. Cloud, Minn.: Rhetoric Society of America, 1968—. 4/yr.

(Formerly *Rhetoric Society Newsletter*, 1968–75.)

Carries an annual "Current Bibliography of Books on Rhetoric."

(D377) *Bibliographic Annual in Speech Communication.* This and its predecessor listed North American books and articles on rhetoric and public address for 1950–74.

COMPUTERS

D101 *Computers and the Humanities.* Elmsford, N.Y.: Pergamon, 1966—. 6/yr.

Carries an annual, international, classified bibliography of books, articles, and dissertations; categories include archaeology, history, language and literature, and music.

A "Directory of Scholars Active" is a triannual list of work in progress in the humanities involving computers.

Each issue carries abstracts and brief notices of selected books and articles.

(A1) *MLA International Bibliography.*

Studies on computer-assisted research in language and literature are listed in Vol. I under General Literature and Related Topics. IV. Themes and Types.

(B1) *Annual Bibliography of English Language and Literature.*

See Language, Literature, and the Computer, Vol. 46, 1971—.

CREATIVE WRITING

This very selective listing covers mainly North American writing. See also the lists under little magazines and small presses, below, and these general periodical indexes: *Arts and Humanities Citation Index* (A6), *Humanities Index* (A8),

American Humanities Index (A9), *British Humanities Index* (A10), and *Reader's Guide to Periodical Literature* (A26).

A. Poetry

D105 *Index of American Periodical Verse.* Metuchen, N.J.: Scarecrow, 1971—. Annual.

An author and title index to current poetry published in about 200 North American periodicals.

D106 *Anthology of Magazine Verse & Yearbook of American Poetry.* Beverly Hills, Calif.: Monitor Book, 1980—. Annual.

The yearbook section, for 1979—, lists U.S. and Canadian books of poetry, biography, and criticism, and lists publishers and poetry magazines, poetry societies and organizations, and poetry prizes.

Earlier editions of this title provided comparable coverage for 1913–41. William Stanley Braithwaite, ed., *Anthology of Magazine Verse and Yearbook of American Poetry* (various publishers and places, 1913–29, 1959); *Anthology of Magazine Verse for 1931–1934* (New York: Praebar, 1932–35); Alan F. Pater, ed., *Anthology of Magazine Verse and Yearbook of American Poetry* (New York: various publishers, 1936–42).

B. Fiction

D110 *Short Story Index.* New York: Wilson, 1953—. Annual, with five-year cumulations.

An author, title, and subject index to current and older short stories published in collections and in 45 periodicals indexed by the *Reader's Guide* (A26) and the *Humanities Index* (A8). Continues the *Index to Short Stories* (New York: Wilson, 1915–36).

D111 *Best American Short Stories.* Boston: Houghton Mifflin, 1915—. Annual.

(Titled *Best Short Stories,* 1915–41. All volumes include the *Yearbook of the American Short Story.*)

Most volumes have included, variously, an extensive list of the year's American short stories, a "Roll of Honor" (selective list of stories), and lists of magazines and anthologies.

D112 *Fiction Index.* London: Assn. of Assistant Librarians, 1953—. Irregular.

A subject list of current and older volumes of English language fiction.

D113 *Fiction Catalog.* New York: Wilson, 1901—. Irregular.

A selective, author, title, and subject list of current and older English language fiction. The ninth edition was published in 1976.

D114 *Armchair Detective: A Quarterly Journal Devoted to the Appreciation of Mystery, Detective, and Suspense Fiction.* Del Mar, Calif., Publisher's, 1967—. 4/yr.

"A Checklist of Mystery, Detective, and Suspense Fiction Published in the U.S." appears in each issue.

D115 *Best Detective Stories of the Year.* New York: Dutton, 1945—. Annual.

Includes "The Yearbook of the Detective Story," for 1962— (in 1963—), a selective list of collections, anthologies, books of criticism and biography, necrology, and "honor roll" of the year's stories.

D116 *International Science Fiction Yearbook.* New York: Quick Fox, 1979—; London: Pierrot, 1978—. Annual.

A bibliographic annual with chapters on the year's book output, prizes, libraries and collections, magazines, film, radio, and television.

(D355) *Science Fiction Chronicle.*
Each issue includes a publisher list of new science fiction books.

(D352) *The N.E.S.F.A. Index: Science Fiction Magazines and Original Anthologies.*
An annual list of current science fiction short stories.

(D354) *Science Fiction and Fantasy Book Review.*
Attempts to review most of the year's 1,000-1,500 English-language science fiction and fantasy books.

C. Drama

D118 *Play Index.* New York: Wilson, 1949—. Irregular.
An author, title, subject, and cast index to current and older published plays.

D119 *Best Plays of* [year]. New York: Dodd, Mead, 1899—. Annual.
Covers 1894—. In addition to printing excerpts from several Broadway plays, this lists drama performances in New York and other U.S. cities, and provides information on runs, casts, awards, and recordings.

CRITICAL AND LITERARY THEORY

Although no single bibliography is devoted exclusively to this subject, the major literary bibliographies do include sections specifically listing studies on the theory of literature and literary criticism. See also *Bulletin Signalétique* (A2), *LLINQUA: Language and Literature Index Quarterly* (A3), and *Abstracts of English Studies* (B3) and these indexes: *Arts and Humanities Citation Index* (A6), *Humanities Index* (A8), *American Humanities Index* (A9), *British Humanities Index* (A10), and *Essay and General Literature Index* (A2). See also bibliographies on art and aesthetics, comparative literature, philosophy, and social sciences.

(A1) *MLA International Bibliography.*
Studies on literary and critical theory in general are listed in Vol. I under General Literature and Related Topics. II. Literary Criticism and Literary Theory. Additional relevant items are listed under Literature, General and Comparative, under Themes and Types, under the various English and American literary period sections, and under sections for national literatures in Vol. II.

(D80) *Canadian Review of Comparative Literature.*
See "Revue des Revues" for an annual list of articles on literary theory and critical methodology.

(B1) *Annual Bibliography of English Language and Literature.*
A major section lists studies on literary history and criticism, with subsections for studies of genres and versification. Prior to Vol. 48, 1973, this section was titled Literature, General, and had subsections for literary history, literary criticism, and meter.

(B72) *American Literary Scholarship.*
The chapter "Themes, Topics, Criticism" reviews the year's American studies in critical and literary theory; subheadings include, for example, Theory of Fiction and Structuralism and Semiology.

(C11) *Bibliographie der französischen Literaturwissenschaft.*
Studies in critical theory and methods and in literary history are listed under "Critique et Méthodes," "Theorie du Texte," and "Structuralisme" in Chapter i.

(C61) *Bibliographie der deutschen Sprach- und Literaturwissenschaft.*
Chapter v, "Allgemeine Literaturwissenschaft," lists studies on literary criticism and theory.

D121 *Structuralist Review: A Journal of Theory, Criticism, and Pedagogy.*
New York: Queens College Press, 1978—. 3/yr.
Carries an annual bibliography of structuralist criticism and theory.

D122 *Structuralist Research Information.* Nashville, Tenn.: Vanderbilt Univ., 1978—. Irregular.
Each issue carries news of interest to structuralists and semioticians and provides an annotated list of international dissertations, books, and articles. These materials, some unpublished, are available from the Structuralist Research Group at Vanderbilt University.

DISSERTATIONS AND THESES

The list here is selective; several bibliographies in Chapters iii and iv also list dissertations on specific literatures. Theses are, in general, poorly served by existing bibliographies.

A. American and Canadian

D128 *Dissertation Abstracts International.* Ann Arbor: University Microfilms International, 1938—. 12/yr.
A monthly, classified compilation of abstracts of most, but not all, North American doctoral dissertations, with subject (permuted title) and author indexes in each issue and an annual cumulated author index. The first issue included dissertations completed in 1935–38; coverage for the first years was very selective. Section A covers the social sciences and humanities. Section C covers foreign dissertations, selectively. Within each subject division, dissertations are listed alphabetically by author. Information provided: author, title, length, director, school, date, and abstract.

D129 *Comprehensive Dissertation Index.* Ann Arbor: University Microfilms International, 1973—. Annual.
An annual subject (permuted title) and author index to North American dissertations, 1861—. Keyed to abstracts in *Dissertation Abstracts International* and to listings in *American Doctoral Dissertations* and other dissertation bibliographies. The initial 37-volume set (1973) had separate volumes for major subject areas, and each of the annual supplements consists of five volumes, one an author index and the other four subject indexes. Literature, linguistics, and language dissertations are listed in Vol. IV, Part II.

D130 *American Doctoral Dissertations.* Ann Arbor: University Microfilms International, 1934—. Annual.
Lists most doctoral dissertations accepted by American and Canadian universities. Arranged by subject, then university, then author. Author index.

D131 *The Gypsy Scholar: A Graduate Forum for Literary Criticism.* East Lansing: Michigan State Univ. 1973—. 3/yr.

"Bibliography of Doctoral Dissertations in British and American Literature," for 1974—, is a classified list of about 70% of the year's American dissertations. Author index.

D132 *Master's Theses in the Arts and Social Sciences.* Cedar Falls, Iowa: Research Publications, 1977—. Annual.

Provides a classified list of U.S. and Canadian theses, for 1976—. Author and institution indexes.

D133 *Master's Abstracts: A Catalog of Selected Master's Theses on Microfilm.* Ann Arbor: University Microfilms International, 1962—. 4/yr.

A selective classified list of abstracts of master's theses from about 90 universities. The author and subject index in each issue is cumulated annually.

B. European

(D128) *Dissertation Abstracts International*, Section C.

D134 *Répertoire des Thèses de Doctorat Européenees.* Louvain: Dewallens, 1970—. Annual.

An author index to West European doctoral dissertations (excluding Spain, Portugal, Italy, and East Germany). Entries are arranged under three broad subject areas: humanities, medicine, and science.

D135 *Index to Theses Accepted for Higher Degrees by the Universities of Great Britain and Ireland and the Council for National Academic Awards.* London: ASLIB, 1950—. Annual.

A classified list of doctoral dissertations, with author and subject indexes. Information provided: author, title, degree, university, date.

D136 *Titles of Dissertations Approved for the Ph.D., M.Sc., and M. Litt. Degrees in the University of Cambridge.* Cambridge: Cambridge Univ. Press, 1958—. Annual.

An author list of Cambridge dissertations, arranged under the faculties for whom the student worked. Author index.

Continues *Abstracts of Dissertations Approved for the Ph.D., M.Sc., and M. Litt. Degrees in the University of Cambridge* (Cambridge: Cambridge Univ. Press, 1927–59).

D137 *Successful Candidates for the Degree of D. Phil., B. Litt., and B.Sc., with Titles of Their Theses.* Oxford: Oxford Univ. Press, 1950—. Annual.

A classified and author list of Oxford dissertations. Authors and titles are listed by subject areas. Author index.

Continues *Abstracts of Dissertations for the Degree of Doctor of Philosophy*, 13 vols. (Oxford: Oxford Univ. Prss, 1925–40).

D138 *Catalogue des Thèses de Doctorat Soutenues devant les Universités Françaises.* Paris: Cercle de la Librairie, 1884—. Annual.

A classified list of French university dissertations with author, subject, and university indexes. Entries list author, title, pagination, and university and frequently note whether there is a bibliography in the dissertation.

D139 *Jahresverzeichnis der Hochschulschriften der DDR, der BRD und Westberlins.* Leipzig: VEB Verlag fur Büch- and Bibliothekwesen, 1885—. Annual.

German dissertations are listed by university, with author and detailed subject indexes.

D140 *Gesamtverzeichnis österreichischer Dissertationen.* Vienna: Verband der Wissenschaftlichen Gesellschaften Österreichs, 1967—. Annual.
    Dissertations are listed by university and then by school or faculty. Author and subject indexes.

D141 *Jahresverzeichnis der schweizerische Hochschulschriften.* Basel: Verlag der Universitätsbibliothek, 1898—. Annual.
    Dissertations, and also faculty books and articles, are listed by university and then by faculty; author and subject indexes are included (the latter until 1973).

DON JUAN THEME

D145 *West Virginia University Bulletin: Philological Papers.* Morgantown: West Virginia Univ., 1936—. Irregular.
    Bibliographies in papers Nos. 15 (1966), 17 (1970), 20 (1973), 23 (1975), and 26 (Supplement 1980) supplement the Singer bibliography: Armand E. Singer, *The Don Juan Theme, Versions and Criticism: A Bibliography* (Morgantown: West Virginia Univ. Press, 1965).

DRAMA

The bibliographies listed here cover studies of drama as a genre and of specific plays, dramatists, and drama topics. See also most of the period and national literature bibliographies in which there are often subsections for drama. For bibliographies of plays, see Creative Writing, Drama, above.

(A1) *MLA International Bibliography.*
    Studies on drama as a genre and in general are listed under individual national literatures and literary periods in Vols. I and II, and under General Literature and Related Topics. IV. Themes and Types in Vol. I.

(B1) *Annual Bibliography of English Language and Literature.*
    Studies on drama and theater history are listed in the chapter on literary history and criticism. Vol. 43—, 1968—; the chapters for literary periods each include a subsection for drama and theater.

D150 *Revue d'Histoire du Théâtre.* Paris: La Société d'Histoire du Théâtre, 1948—. 4/yr.
    Carries an annual, international, comprehensive, and classified bibliography of books and articles on most aspects of the theater except stagecraft. About 1,800 periodicals are scanned for articles on theory, history, literary aspects, and types of drama. The bibliography appeared in each issue, 1948–65, and annually thereafter.

D151 *Modern Drama.* Toronto: Univ. of Toronto, 1958—. 4/yr.
    "Modern Drama Studies: An Annual Bibliography," 1972— (Vol. 17—, 1974—), is an annual, classified, international list of books and articles on areas, topics, and figures (playwrights and influential men and women other than performers) in modern drama since 1900. Covers drama of the U.S.A., Great Britain, the Commonwealth, Germany, France, Italy, Spain (including Portugal and Latin America), Scandinavia, East Europe and the U.S.S.R., and Asia (Near East, Israel, Far East, South Asia).
    "Modern Drama: A Selective Bibliography of Works Published in English," 1959–67 (Vol. 3–11, 1960–68), covered the same subject areas but a more limited range of publications.

D152 *Theatre/Drama Abstracts.* Pleasant Hill, Calif.: Theatre/Drama and Speech Information Center, 1975–80.
(Titled *Theatre/Drama & Speech Index*, 1974. See D376.)
An international, comprehensive abstracting service for articles, 1974–77. Author and subject index.

(B59) *Nineteenth Century Theatre Research.*
Carries a bibliography of studies of 19th-century British theater.

(B44) *Restoration and Eighteenth Century Theatre Research.*
Carries a bibliography of studies of British theater of the period.

D153 *New York Theatre Critics' Reviews.* New York: Critics' Theatre Reviews, 1940—. 52/yr.
A weekly compilation of reviews of New York theater productions (premiers, long-running productions, and revivals) from six newspapers, two weekly news magazines, and two broadcast network review services. Title index and an index of authors, producers, directors, composers and lyricists, set designers, choreographers, costume designers, and cast.

D154 *Annotated Bibliography of New Publications in the Performing Arts.* New York: Drama Bookshop, 1971—. 4/yr.
A classified bibliography of new books, mainly in English, on theater and other performing arts, including television, radio, film, musicals, and the circus.
This supplements *Performing Arts Books in Print: An Annotated Bibliography* (New York: Drama Book Specialists, 1973).

D155 *Bibliographic Guide to Theatre Arts.* Boston: Hall, 1976—. Annual.
An annual, international, comprehensive bibliography of all publications cataloged by the New York Public Library, supplemented by entries from Library of Congress cataloging, 1975—. Items listed by author, title, and subject.

D156 *Theater Journal.* Washington, D.C.: American Theatre Assn., 1949—. 4/yr.
(Titled *Educational Theatre Journal*, 1949–78.)
"Doctoral Projects in Progress in Theatre Arts" is an annual list of dissertation projects, 1952— (Vol. 5—, 1953—). Items are arranged under broad headings, such as Africa, nineteenth-century England, and criticism and audiences.
"Scholarly Works in Progress," 1974—, is an annual list of studies and translations in press or in progress.

(C66) *Maske und Kothurn.*
Although mainly a bibliography of studies on the German theater, this lists some items on international theater biography, history, bibliography, and stagecraft.

ECONOMICS AND BUSINESS

The following bibliographies cover the whole field of economics, finance, and business and provide access to current information about publishing, financial programs and conditions affecting literature, and other literary matters relating to business and finance. See also standard newspaper indexes such as the *Wall Street Journal Index* and the *New York Times Index*.

D160 *Business Periodicals Index.* New York: Wilson, 1958—. 11/yr., with annual cumulation.

A subject and author index to articles on all aspects of business. Useful subject headings include communication, fiction, literary agents, and publishing. Covers mainly North American periodicals.

D161 *International Bibliography of Economics.* Paris: UNESCO, 1955—. Annual. (Part of the *International Bibliography of the Social Sciences* series.)

An annual, international, comprehensive, and classified bibliography of books and articles on all aspects of economics. Subject and author indexes.

EDUCATION

Education bibliographies list items on educational theory and research as well as on practical classroom techniques and methods. See also the sections for composition and rhetoric and language, linguistics, and language teaching.

D165 *Current Index to Journals in Education.* Phoenix, Ariz.: Oryx, 1969—. 12/yr., with biannual cumulations.

An international, comprehensive index to articles in about 750 English language periodicals. Organized into four parts: abstracts, subject index, author index, and tables of contents of indexed journals. *CIJE* lists articles on such subjects as teaching methods and syllabi, literary criticism and bibliographies, literary genres and subjects, writing and journalism, specific writers, genres, and themes, etc., as well as on educational issues, developments, research, and methods.

D166 *Education Index.* New York: Wilson, 1932—. 10/yr., with annual cumulation.

An author and subject index to about 350 North American English language periodicals, related yearbooks, and some monographs, for 1929—. Coverage includes teaching methods, literary criticism, genres, bibliographies.

(A15) *Resources in Education.*

Unpublished papers in the ERIC system are abstracted and indexed.

(D96) *Research in the Teaching of English.*

See the biannual bibliography.

D167 *British Education Index.* London: British Library, 1961—. 4/yr.

Indexes articles in about 175 periodicals published or distributed in Great Britain, for 1954—. Author and two subject indexes.

D168 *Bulletin Signalétique 520: Sciences de l'Éducation.* Paris: Centre National de la Recherche Scientifique, 1948—. 4/yr.

Classified bibliography of articles from about 750 international periodicals. Author and subject indexes in each issue and cumulated annually.

(D256) *Language Teaching and Linguistics: Abstracts.*

Covers articles on language, language learning, and language teaching.

(D257) *ACTFL Annual Bibliography of Books and Articles on Pedagogy in Foreign Languages.*

Covers books and articles on foreign language teaching.

ETHNIC STUDIES

See sections in this chapter for black studies, Jewish studies, folklore, popular culture, and regionalism (U.S.A.); also see under American literature (Ch. iii) and under the general indexes and bibliographies (Ch. ii). The *MLA International Bibliography* (A1) includes headings for Afro-American, American Indian, and Mexican-American studies in the American literature sections.

D170 *Chicano Studies Periodical Index.** Berkeley, Calif.: Univ. of California, Chicano Studies Library, 1978—. 2/yr.

D171 *Index to Literature on the American Indian.* San Francisco: Indian Historian Press, 1970—. Irregular.

An author and subject list of books and articles on or by Native Americans. Covers a wide range of subjects (such as games, agriculture, technology) in both scholarly and popular publications. See also *Western American Literature* (D331).

EXPLICATION

See also the literary genre sections of this chapter, the general indexes and bibliographies (Ch. ii), period bibliographies (Ch. iii), national literature bibliographies (Ch. iv), and author bibliographies (Ch. vi).

D175 *Explicator.* Washington, D.C.: Heldref, 1942—. 4/yr.

"Checklist of Explication" annually lists explication of mainly English language writing published in books and articles. A separate annual index lists explication published in *Explicator*.

FICTION

Although several journals—chiefly *Modern Fiction Studies, Critique: Studies in Modern Fiction*, and *Studies in the Novel*—regularly publish bibliographical articles on specific aspects of fiction, there is no single, general bibliography of studies of long fiction. Short fiction scholarship, however, is recorded in *Studies in Short Fiction*. See also sections in this chapter for comparative literature, folklore, popular culture, and science fiction; see general and period bibliographies in Chapters iii and iv; see relevant author bibliographies in Chapter vi.

D180 *Modern Fiction Studies.* West Lafayette, Ind.: Purdue Univ., 1955—. 4/yr.

"Recent Books on Modern Fiction," 1955—, is a biannual checklist and review article on recent, international books dealing with modern fiction in general and with individual authors. Titled "Modern Fiction Newsletter" in Vols. 1–14.

D181 *Studies in Short Fiction.* Newberry, S.C.: Newberry College, 1963—. 4/yr.

Carries an annual list of short story criticism (books and articles), with items arranged under the names of subject authors.

These annual bibliographies have been augmented and cumulated in: Warren S. Walker, comp., *Twentieth-Century Short Story Explication: Interpretations 1900-1975, of Short Fiction Since 1800*, 3d ed. (Hamden, Conn.: Shoe String, 1977; supplement, 1980).

(A1) *MLA International Bibliography.*
Studies of prose fiction are listed in Vol. I under General Literature and Related Topics. IV. Themes and Types, and under national literatures and literary periods in Vols. I and II. Coverage includes studies of fiction as a genre, science fiction, popular fiction types, and related critical issues.

(B1) *Annual Bibliography of English Language and Literature.*
Studies on fiction as a genre are listed under Literary History and Criticism, Vol. 43, 1968—.

D182 *Gothic: The Review of Supernatural Horror Fiction.* * Baton Rouge: Gothic, 1979—. 2/yr.
Carries an annual bibliography of criticism of Gothic fiction.

D183 *Studies in the Novel.* Denton: North Texas State Univ., 1969—. 4/yr.
Regularly carries review articles on recent fiction criticism.

FILM

The general periodical indexes (A6–A27) cover film studies and reviews, although indexing terms vary from "cinema" to "film" to "motion pictures" or "moving pictures." See also the *Art Index* (D6) and *Contemporary Literary Criticism* (B67). The titles listed here tend to stress film studies more than film reviews.

D190 *Film Literature Index.* Albany, N.Y.: Filmdex, 1973—. 4/yr.
An author and subject index to international periodicals; subject headings include names, film titles, film genres, and topics in filmmaking, film criticism, and film study. Film reviews are also listed.

D191 *International Index to Film Periodicals: An Annotated Guide.* New York: St. Martin's, 1972—. Annual.
An international, classified bibliography of articles in about 80 periodicals on all aspects of film, including film industry, distribution, society and cinema, aesthetics, history, individual films, biography, and institutions, festivals, and conferences. Author, subject, and director indexes.

(A1) *MLA International Bibliography.*
Studies on film are listed under a subsection for cinema in Vol. I., General Literature and Related Topics. IV. Themes and Types.

(B65) *Journal of Modern Literature.*
The annual Modernist bibliography, 1970—, includes a section of studies of film as literature.

(C24) *French XX Bibliography.*
Part III, Vol. 20, 1968—, covers international books, articles, and dissertations on French film, with a subsection for general studies and for studies of specific directors and writers. Prior to Vol. 20, film studies were listed under Theatre and Cinema. Film reviews are included.

(C11) *Bibliographie der französischen Literaturwissenschaft.*
Studies on general issues (including film and literature) and specific individuals in French filmmaking are listed under I. Généralités. Cinema, 1956/58—.

D192 *Film Review Digest Annual.* Millwood, N.Y.: KTO, 1976—. Annual.
Provides excerpts from North American and British reviews of international feature-length films, for 1975—.

FOLKLORE

Bibliographies listed here cover folklore in general or American, Irish, Scottish, or British specifically. See also the major national literature bibliographies (Ch. iv) and the sections in this chapter for art and aesthetics, history, linguistics, music, names, popular culture, regionalism (U.S.A.), and social sciences.

(A1) *MLA International Bibliography.*
International folklore studies are listed in Vol. I; additional studies are listed in Vol. II under Modern Greek, African, and East European literature sections. The main folklore bibliography includes sections for prose narratives, gnomic folklore, folk poetry, folk games and toys, dramatic folklore, music and dance, folk customs, beliefs, and symbolism, and material culture. Prior to 1970 folklore studies were listed under General Literature and Related Topics.

D195 *Internationale Volkskundliche Bibliographie/International Folklore and Folklife Bibliography/Bibliographie Internationale des Arts et Traditions Populaires.* Bonn: Habelt, 1949—. Annual.
An international, classified bibliography of books and articles, for 1939—, on folklore. Coverage is comparable with that of the *MLA International Bibliography.* Author and subject indexes.
Continues *Volkskundliche Bibliographie* (Berlin: de Gruyter, 1917–41).

D196 *Demos: Internationale Ethnographische und Folkloristische Informationen.* Berlin: Akademie der Wissenschaften der DDR, 1960—. 4/yr.
A classified, annotated bibliography of books and articles on ethnology and folklore. Annual author, book review, and periodical index. Covers international folklore but lists mainly East European publications.

D197 *Folklore Bibliography for* [year]. Philadelphia: Inst. for the Study of Human Issues, 1979—. Annual.
An international bibliography of books and articles on all aspects of the folklore of the Western Hemisphere, including the Spanish- and Portuguese-speaking nations. Continues coverage for 1973–74 in *Indiana Folklore Institute Monograph Series,* Vols. 28 and 29 (Bloomington, Ind.: Research Center for Language and Semiotic Studies, 1973, 1974), and for 1937–72 in *Southern Folklore Quarterly* (Gainesville: Univ. of Florida, 1938–73).

(B1) *Annual Bibliography of English Language and Literature.*
Studies on the folklore of the British Isles are listed in a separate section, Vol. 48—, 1973—. Prior to this, a few folklore studies were listed under Auxiliary Studies, Vols. 15–47, 1934–72.

(B72) *American Literary Scholarship.*
The year's studies in American folklore were reviewed for 1965–74.

D198 *Journal of American Folklore.* Washington, D.C.: American Folklore Soc. 1888—. 4/yr.
"Work in Progress" is an annual list of scholarly projects, including dissertations, 1960—.
An annual, international, classified bibliography of books and articles, 1954–62 (Vol. 68–76, 1955–63), was published as a supplement; it was superseded by coverage in *Abstracts of Folklore Studies.*

D199 *Abstracts of Folklore Studies.* Austin, Texas: American Folklore Soc. 1963–75. 4/yr.

Abstracts of international articles on international folklore were listed by periodical title, and there was an annual subject index.

(C43) *Revista de Dialectología y Tradiciones Populares.*

An annual bibliography includes studies of folklore in Spain and Spanish-speaking America.

GOVERNMENT PUBLICATIONS

The U.S. government publishes, or sponsors the publication of, an incredible range of materials, including a not inconsiderable amount of interest to literary scholars. Bibliographies, exhibit catalogs, lectures, books and pamphlets, and information about national historical monuments and sites (which include homes of writers and artists), as well as the many official reports, announcements, and regulations of such federal agencies as the National Endowment for the Humanities, are listed.

D205 *Monthly Catalog of United States Government Publications.* Washington, D.C.: GPO, 1895—. 12/yr.

Each issue lists documents published by all branches of the government; arranged by department, bureau, or agency, with a subject index.

Cumulated: *Cumulative Subject Index to the Monthly Catalog of United States Government Publications, 1900–71* (Washington, D.C.: Carrollton, 1973).

D206 *Index to U.S. Government Periodicals.* Chicago: Infordata, 1975—. 4/yr.

An author and subject index, for 1970—, to about 160 U.S. Government periodicals.

D207 *CIS/Index to Publications of the United States Congress.* Washington, D.C.: Congressional Information Service, 1971—. 12/yr.

An author and subject index to Congressional publications, such as House and Senate committee hearings, reports, and documents.

HISTORY, POLITICAL SCIENCE, AND LAW

The items listed here emphasize English and American history, government, and law. The major period bibliographies (Ch. iii) should also be consulted, as should appropriate sections of Chapter iv (the non-English literatures) and of this chapter, such as classical literature, philosophy, and social sciences.

(B1) *Annual Bibliography of English Language and Literature.*

"Related Historical Studies" are listed under the divisions for the 16th through 20th centuries, Vol. 46—, 1971—.

D210 *Historical Abstracts: Bibliography of the World's Periodical Literature.* Santa Barbara, Calif.: American Bibliographic Center/Clio Press, 1955—. 4/yr.

"Part A. Modern History Abstracts, 1450–1914": Vol. 17—, 1971—.

"Part B. Twentieth-Century Abstracts": Vol 17—, 1971—.

An international, comprehensive, classified bibliography of articles (with abstracts). In three parts: general (methodology, historiography, teaching, and study), topics (such as international relations, social and cultural history, science and technology), and areas or countries. Studies on the U.S.A. and Canada have been excluded starting with Vol. 16, 1970. Issues Nos. 1 and 2 have their own index and issue No. 4 is an annual cumulated subject and author index.

D211 *America: History and Life.* Santa Barbara, Calif.: American Bibliographic Center/Clio Press, 1964—. 7/yr.

An international, comprehensive, classified bibliography, with abstracts, of books, reviews, articles, and dissertations on the U.S.A. and Canada. Now in four parts: article abstracts (three issues per year), book reviews (two issues per year), bibliography of books, articles, and dissertations, and an annual detailed subject and author index.

D212 *Annual Bibliography of British and Irish History.* London: Harvester, 1976—. Annual.

An international, classified bibliography of books and articles, 1975—, on the history of Britain, Ireland, medieval Wales, and Scotland before the union. Items arranged by period. Author and subject indexes.

D213 *History: Reviews of New Books.* Washington, D.C.: Heldref, 1972—. 10/yr.

A book review journal with reviews arranged under headings for Europe, Asia, General, and America. Author index in each issue, but not cumulated.

D214 *International Political Science Abstracts/Documentation Politique Internationale.* Paris: International Political Science Assn., 1951—. 6/yr.

An international, classified bibliography (with abstracts) of articles on political science. Each issue has a subject index, and there is an annual author and subject index. Classification scheme: methods and theory, thinkers and ideas, governmental and administrative institutions, political process, international relations, national and area studies.

D215 *Perspective: Monthly Reviews of New Books on Government, Politics, International Affairs.* Washington, D.C.: Heldref, 1972—. 10/yr.

A book review journal with reviews listed under sections for United States, Asia, Africa and the Middle East, western hemisphere, comparative politics, international relations, and Europe and the U.S.S.R. Author index in each issue and cumulated annually.

D216 *Index to Legal Periodicals.* New York: Wilson, 1909—. 11/yr.

An author and subject index to major articles in about 400 North American, United Kingdom, and Commonwealth journals. Book review index and table of cases included.

HUMOR

D220 *American Humor: An Interdisciplinary Newsletter.* Richmond, Va.: American Humor Studies Assn., 1974—. 2/yr.

"Criticism on American Humor: An Annotated Checklist" is an annual feature that lists articles and dissertations on American humor in literature, folklore, popular culture, mass media, education, and other areas of American culture.

IRISH LITERATURE

See also the section for Celtic studies.

D225 *Études Irlandaises.* Lille: Centre d'Études et de Recherches Irlandaises, 1972—. Annual.

"The Year's Work in Anglo-Irish Literature" is an annual, international list of books and articles about Anglo-Irish writing and includes a list of current creative writing. Comparable coverage for 1970–72 was carried in the *Irish University Review: A Journal of Irish Studies* (Shannon: Irish Univ. Press, 1970–72).

JEWISH STUDIES
See also Ethnic Studies, above.

D230 *Jewish Book Annual.* New York: Jewish Book Council, 1942—. Annual.
A review of Jewish books, chiefly North American, on such matters as juvenile literature, women, individual writers, and bibliographical subjects. Selective, annotated bibliographies of current Jewish fiction, nonfiction, juveniles, Yiddish, Israeli, Anglo-Jewish, and award-winning Jewish books.

D231 *Index to Jewish Periodicals.* Cleveland Heights, Ohio: Index to Jewish Periodicals, 1963—. 4/yr.
An author and subject index to about fifty English-language periodicals of general and scholarly interest.

(A1) *MLA International Bibliography.*
Lists studies on Yiddish literature, 1951—. For 1951–54, listed under East European literature; for 1955, listed separately; for 1956—, listed under Germanic literature, Vol. II.

JOURNALISM AND MASS COMMUNICATION
See also the sections on periodicals and on speech, below.

D235 *Journalism Quarterly: Devoted to Research in Mass Communication.* Athens, Ohio: Assn. for Education in Journalism, 1924—. 4/yr.
"Articles on Mass Communication in U. S. and Foreign Journals: A Selected Annotated Bibliography," 1930—, is an international, classified, and quarterly list of articles. Subjects covered: advertising, audience and communicator analysis, broadcasting, communication theory, community journalism, courts and law, criticism and defense of media, editorial policy and methods, education for journalism, government and media, history and biography, research methods, and technology.

D236 *Communication Abstracts: An International Information Service.* Beverly Hills, Calif.: Sage, 1978—. 4/yr.
A classified bibliography, with abstracts, of articles on communication in about 80 English language journals. Author and subject indexes.

(D377) *Bibliographic Annual in Speech Communication.*
"Studies in Mass Communication: A Selected Bibliography," for 1972–74 (Vols. 4–6, 1974–75) was a comprehensive, classified, and international list of books and articles on mass communication and of interest to scholars in radio-television, journalism, speech, and mass communication.

D237 *Communication Yearbook.* New Brunswick, N.J.: International Communication Assn., 1977—. Annual.
A bibliographic review with chapters surveying recent work in information systems and in interpersonal, mass, organizational, intercultural, political, instructional, and health communications. Subject and author indexes.

(D23) *ABHB. Annual Bibliography of the History of the Printed Book and Libraries.*
   The section on newspapers and journalism lists books and articles, 1970—.

D238 *Journalism Abstracts.* Minneapolis, Minn.: Assn. for Education in Journalism, 1963—. Annual.
   An annual author list of abstracts of master's theses and doctoral dissertations written in U.S. universities. Subject index.

(D367) *Bulletin Signalétique 521: Sociologie, Ethnologie.*
   The section "Sociologie de la Communication et des Mass Media" is an international, comprehensive bibliography of current articles.

LIBRARIES

Bibliographies that list studies of, or information about, collections and recent library acquisitions are listed here, as well as bibliographies with studies in library and information science. Most major libraries publish a newsletter or journal in which significant acquisitions are listed and collections described; *Library Literature* indexes these. See also the sections in this chapter for journalism and mass communication, manuscripts, and reference books.

D245 *Library Literature: An Index to Library and Information Science.* New York: Wilson, 1921—. 6/yr.
   A comprehensive and international author and subject index to periodicals, books, and pamphlets dealing with libraries, library collections, librarianship, and information science, including issues involving archives, manuscripts, collections, bibliographic control, communications, and censorship.

D246 *Library and Information Science Abstracts.* London: Library Assn., 1969—. 6/yr.
   (Supersedes *Library Science Abstracts,* 1950–68.)
   An international, classified compilation of abstracts of articles on bibliography, collections, manuscripts, and archives. Annual author and subject index.

D247 *CALL: Current Awareness Library Literature.* Framingham, Mass.: Goldstein Associates, 1972–74, 1976—. 6/yr.
   Classified arrangement of tables of contents of current international library periodicals and newsletters. Abstracts selected current articles.

(D23) *ABHB: Annual Bibliography of the History of the Printed Book and Libraries.*
   An international, comprehensive, and classified bibliography of books and articles, for 1970—, about institutions, libraries, librarianship, and scholarship.

D248 *Journal of Library History, Philosophy, and Comparative Librarianship.* Austin: Univ. of Texas Press, 1966—. 4/yr.
   "The Year's Work in American Library History," for 1967— (in Vol. 3, 1968—), is an annual evaluative review essay citing books, articles, and dissertations.

LINGUISTICS, LANGUAGE, AND LANGUAGE TEACHING

Many of the bibliographies listed in Chapter iv (on the non-English literatures) include language studies and language teaching items. Other relevant sections in this chapter are on comparative literature, composition, computers, education, folklore, journalism and mass communication, and style. The *Arts and Humanities Citation Index* (A6) covers journals that emphasize historical and analytical linguistics, language, and philology, while the *Social Sciences Citation Index* (D366) covers journals dealing with psycho- and sociolinguistics.

D251   *Linguistics Bibliography for the Year [date]/Bibliographie Linguistique de l'Année.* Utrecht: Spectrum, 1947—. Annual.

An annual, international, comprehensive classified bibliography of books, reviews, and articles, 1939—. Headings include bibliography, general linguistics and related fields of study (such as stylistics, translation, psycholinguistics, and onomastics), and the major language groups. No author or subject indexes.

(A1)   *MLA International Bibliography.*

Covers all aspects of linguistics including theoretical, descriptive, and comparative linguistics, and the language families. The separate section for linguistics began with the 1968 bibliography and is now Vol. III; prior to 1968 linguistics coverage was included under the separate sections for individual literatures.

The ACTFL Annual Bibliography of Books and Articles on Pedagogy in Foreign Languages (D257) for 1969–72 was carried as Vol. IV of the MLA bibliography for the same years.

D252   *Bulletin Signalétique 524: Sciences du Langage.* Paris: Centre National de la Recherche Scientifique, 1948—. 4/yr.

An international, comprehensive, and classified bibliography of books, articles, published proceedings, and works in progress; sections include psycholinguistics, sociolinguistics, linguistic theories, communication, literary semiotics, applied linguistics, and history of linguistics and comparative grammar. Author and subject indexes in each issue are cumulated annually.

D253   *Language and Language Behavior Abstracts.* San Diego, Calif.: Sociological Abstracts, 1967—. 4/yr.

An international, comprehensive, classified bibliography of books, articles, and dissertations on language and language behavior; linguistics studies are not covered, except for psycholinguistics. Among the categories included are verbal learning, stylistics, philosophy of language, speech and hearing, and special education. Items are abstracted. Annual cumulated subject and author indexes, and annual book review index.

D254   *Bibliographie Linguistischer Literatur (BLL): Bibliographie zur allgemeinen Linguistik und zur anglistischen, germanistischen und romanistischen Linguistik.* Frankfurt am Main: Klostermann, 1976—. 4/yr., with annual cumulation.

(Titled *Bibliographie Unselbständiger Literatur—Linguistik*, Vol. 1–3.)

A comprehensive, classified, international bibliography, for years 1971—, of books, articles, published proceedings on German, English, and the Romance languages and linguistics. Author and subject indexes.

(A3)   *LLINQUA: Language and Literature Index Quarterly.*

Quarterly index to articles and book reviews in 500 international periodicals.

D255 *Quarterly Check-List of Linguistics: An International Index of Current Books, Monographs, Brochures, and Separates.* Darien, Conn.: American Bibliographic Service, 1958–72.

An international and comprehensive author list of current books, monographs, etc., and with an annual author, editor, translator index.

(B1) *Annual Bibliography of English Language and Literature.*

Covers books, reviews, and articles on English language, pronunciation, orthography, punctuation, handwriting, vocabulary, and grammar.

(C3) *The Year's Work in Modern Language Studies.*

Carries a chapter on general linguistics, Vol. 35—, 1974—, and the sections on individual languages often include chapters on linguistics studies in those languages.

(D381) *Style.*

The annual bibliography covers language aspects of literature.

D256 *Language Teaching and Linguistics: Abstracts.* London: Cambridge Univ. Press, 1968—. 4/yr.

(Titled *Language-Teaching Abstracts*, Vol. 1–7, 1968–74.)

A classified, international bibliography of abstracts of articles on language, linguistics, and language learning and teaching; biennial author and subject indexes, with those in the fourth issue being cumulative for the volume.

Lists of current research projects in Britain and in Europe appear in alternate issues.

D257 *ACTFL Annual Bibliography of Books and Articles on Pedagogy in Foreign Languages.* New York: American Council on the Teaching of Foreign Languages, 1978—. Annual.

An international, classified bibliography of books and articles, with coverage extending back to 1875. Its publishing history is somewhat complex. Years 1975— published as above; 1974 published in the ERIC system (A15; document no. 125268); 1973 published separately by the ACTFL but also available in the ERIC system (no. 134002); 1967–72 published in *Foreign Language Annals* (New York: ACTFL), with 1969–72 also published as Vol. IV of the *MLA International Bibliography* (A1). Direct predecessors of these were Emma Marie Birkmaier and Dale L. Lange, "A Selective Bibliography on the Teaching of Foreign Languages, 1920–1966," in *Foreign Language Annals*, 1 (1967), 318–53; an "Annotated Bibliography of Modern Language Methodology," for 1915–1959, annually in *Modern Language Journal*, 1–45 (1916–61); James B. Tharp, *Annotated Bibliographies of Modern Language Methodologies for the Years 1946, 1947, 1948* (Columbus: Ohio State Univ. Press, 1952) and Charles H. Handschin, "Work on the Teaching of Modern Languages," for 1875–1912, in *The Teaching of Modern Languages in the United States* (Washington, D.C.: GPO, 1913), pp. 107–49.

LITTLE MAGAZINES AND SMALL PRESSES

Many little magazines are indexed in the general humanities indexes listed in Chapter ii, but the less established titles are not covered adequately, not even by the bibliographies listed here. Retrospective coverage for American little magazines exists: *Index to American Little Magazines, 1900–1919*, 3 vols. (Troy, N.Y.: Whitston, 1974), *Index to American Little Magazines 1920–1939* (Troy, N.Y.:

Whitston, 1969), *Index to Little Magazines 1940–1942* (New York: Johnson, 1967), *Index to Little Magazines 1943–1947* (Denver: Swallow, 1965), and *Index to Little Magazines* (Denver: Swallow, 1949–70). See also items listed on creative writing, above, and periodicals, below.

Small press books present a problem because until 1978 they had not been consistently reviewed or listed in trade bibliographies; now, however, they are reviewed regularly in both *Library Journal* (New York: Bowker) and *Booklist* (Chicago: American Library Association).

A. Little Magazines

D265   *Access to Little Magazines*. Evanston, Ill.: John Gordon Burke, 1977—. Annual.

An author, title, and subject index to about 70 American little magazines, for 1974—. Subject index includes book reviews and interviews.

D266   *Index to Commonwealth Little Magazines*. Troy, N.Y.: Whitston, 1964—. Biennial.

An author and subject index to creative writing, criticism, bibliographical articles, and book reviews in Commonwealth English-language little magazines.

B. Small Presses

D267   *Small Press Review*. Paradise, Calif.: Dustbooks, 1967—. 12/yr.

Reviews new small press books and new little magazines and lists new books and magazines received.

D268   *The American Book Review*. New York: American Book Review, 1978—. 6/yr.

Each issue reviews about 15 books of literature and current thought, mainly published by small, university, regional, and specialist presses.

D269   *Small Press Record of Books*. Paradise, Calif.: Dustbooks, 1969—. Annual.

An author list of small press books in print, with subject, title, and publisher indexes.

D270   *Private Press Books: A Checklist of Books Issued by Private Presses in the Past Year*. Pinner, Eng.: Private Libraries Assn., 1960—. Annual.

Annual list, by publisher, of private press books; author index.

MANUSCRIPTS AND ARCHIVES

Although scholars need information about the locations of manuscripts and archives, as well as studies of them, there is no complete, up-to-date, and continuous inventory. The *National Union Catalog of Manuscript Collections* and the *College and Research Libraries'* annual index are perhaps the most helpful regular bibliographies of North American library holdings. One should also check relevant articles in *American Literary Scholarship* (B72), the two *Year's Work* volumes (B2 and C3), *Resources for American Literary Study* (Richmond, Va.: Virginia Commonwealth Univ.), and Category F of the annual bibliography in *Journal of Modern Literature* (B65), as well as journals and annual reports of major libraries. For studies of individual manuscripts, see the period and author bibliographies. See also bibliographies listed under libraries and under microforms and reprints in this chapter.

D275 *The National Union Catalog of Manuscript Collections.* Washington,
D.C.: Library of Congress, 1959—. Irregular.
 Describes manuscript collections in U.S. libraries and museums that
are open to scholarly researchers. Access is through the biennial subject
and author indexes.
D276 *College and Research Libraries.* Chicago: American Library Assn.,
1939—. 6/yr., with monthly newsletter.
 "News from the Field" in each monthly newsletter notes the acquisi-
tion of books, manuscripts, and collections by U.S. and Canadian libraries; this feature is indexed annually under the heading Acquisitions.
(D245) *Library Literature.*
 See headings for manuscripts, special collections, acquisitions, and
archives.
D277 *American Archivist.* Chicago: Soc. of American Archivists, 1938—. 4/yr.
 "Writings on Archives, Historical Manuscripts, and Current Records," 1942—, is an annual, international bibliography of books, pamphlets, and articles on the management and use of archives, on editing,
and on general issues relating to archives. The emphasis is on historical
rather than strictly literary materials.
D278 *Scriptorium: Revue International des Études Relatives aux Manuscripts.* Antwerp: Standard Boekhandel, 1946—. 2/yr.
 "Bulletin Codicologique" is an international, annotated bibliography
of books and articles about manuscript studies and facsimile editions.
Annotations, usually in the language of the book or article, note which
manuscripts are cited (if any). Generally covers European, medieval
manuscripts.
(D50) *Annual Report of the American Rare, Antiquarian and Out-of-Print
Book Trade.*
 Annual review article on trends in bibliography includes studies in
codicology.

MICROFORMS AND REPRINTS

D280 *Guide to Microforms in Print.* Westport, Conn.: Microform Review,
1961—. Annual.
 An international author, title, and subject list of microforms in print
in all subjects.
D281 *Microform Review.* Westport, Conn.: Microform Review, 1972—. 6/yr.
 "Recent Articles on Micro Publishing," about four times a year, lists
international articles. Omitted in Vol. 4, 1976.
 Each issue carries reviews of microform publications. An author and
title index in each issue is cumulative for the volume.
D282 *Guide to Reprints.* Kent, Conn.: Guide to Reprints, 1967—. Annual.
 An international author and title list of current reprints in print in all
subjects.
D283 *The Reprint Bulletin: Book Reviews.* Dobbs Ferry, N.Y.: Glanville,
1955—. 4/yr.
 Reviews current, reprinted books in all subjects, with the reviews arranged by Dewey classification categories. Covers mainly North American reprint publishers; author index in each issue is cumulative for the
volume.

D284   *Bulletin of Reprints.* Munich: Dokumentation, 1964—. 4/yr.
(Titled *Bibliographia Anastatica*, Vol. 1–10, 1964–73.)
An author, title, and subject list of reprints of international books and serials.
Updates Christa Gnirss, ed., *Internationale Bibliographie der Reprints/International Bibliography of Reprints* (Munich: Dokumentation, 1976).

MUSIC

In addition to their need for current music studies and reviews, literary scholars will be interested in information about librettists, literary-music collaborations, and specific poets and other writers whose work has been set to music.

D290   *Music Index: A Subject-Author Guide to Current Music Periodical Literature.* Detroit: Information Coordinators, 1949—. 12/yr.
An author and subject index to articles on classical, popular, jazz, folk, and ethnic music, on musicology, and on performance and pedagogy; lists reviews of books, performances, and recordings. For literary subjects, see under subject headings for specific authors, literature, genres, themes, and subjects (such as Faust legend).

D291   *RILM Abstracts: Répertoire International de la Littérature Musicale/International Repertory of Music Literature.* New York: International RILM Center, 1967—. 4/yr.
An international, comprehensive, and classified list of abstracts of books, reviews, articles, dissertations, catalogs, and other publications on all aspects of music. There is an author index in each issue and an annual subject index. Relevant classification categories: Poetry and Other Literature in the section on music and other arts and the entire section on ethnomusicology.

NAMES

D295   *Names: Journal of the American Name Society.* Potsdam, N.Y.: American Name Soc. 1953—. 4/yr.
"Bibliography of Personal Names" is an annual, comprehensive, international list of books and articles about worldwide personal names. This updates Elsdon C. Smith, *Personal Names: A Bibliography* (New York: New York Public Library, 1952).
In the same periodical, "Place Name Literature, United States and Canada," 1952—, is a biennial bibliography of books and articles, with most items given a brief summary annotation. This supplements R. B. Sealock and P. A. Seely, *Bibliography of Place Name Literature* (Chicago: American Library Assn., 1948).

D296   *Onoma: Bibliographical and Information Bulletin/Bulletin d'Information et de Bibliographie.* Louvain: International Centre of Onomastics, 1950—. 3/yr.
"Bibliographia Onomastica" is an annual, international, classified bibliography of books and articles on place and person names, with items arranged by subject country.

PERIODICALS

Bibliographies listing studies of periodicals, but not periodical directories, are listed here. See also the sections on little magazines and small presses and on journalism, above.

D301 *Serials Review.* Ann Arbor: Pierian, 1975—. 4/yr.
"Serials Review Index," 1975—, indexes reviews of new, international, and comprehensive periodicals.

(A1) *MLA International Bibliography.*
See the subheading Periodicals under the various literary periods for English, American, and Commonwealth literatures.

(B1) *Annual Bibliography of English Language and Literature.*
"The Newspaper and Periodical," 1973— (Vol. 48—, 1976—), is a subsection under Bibliography.

(B58) *Victorian Periodicals Review.*
Carries an annual checklist of books and articles, 1975—, about Victorian periodicals.

PHILOSOPHY

See also *L'Année Philologique* (D70) for works on Greek and Roman philosophers, and see bibliographies on art and aesthetics, comparative literature, linguistics, critical theory, social sciences, and theology.

D305 *Philosopher's Index: An International Index to Philosophical Periodicals.* Bowling Green, Ohio: Philosophy Documentation Center, 1967—. 4/yr.
An international, comprehensive, selectively abstracted author list of articles. Coverage has been extended back to 1940. Subject index. Book review index.

D306 *Bulletin Signalétique 519: Philosophie.* Paris: Centre National de la Recherche Scientifique, 1948—. 4/yr.
An international, comprehensive, classified bibliography of articles (frequently with brief summaries in French); subject and author indexes in each issue and in a separate, cumulated annual supplement.

D307 *Bibliographie de la Philosophie/Bibliography of Philosophy.* Paris: Vrin, 1937—. 4/yr.
An international, comprehensive, and classified bibliography of books (with annotations, usually in language of the book). Categories include logic, semantics, philosophy of science, philosophical psychology, aesthetics, ethics, social philosophy, philosophy of history, philosophy of religion, history of philosophy, annuals, reference books. Author, subject, and publisher indexes appear in every fourth issue.

D308 *Répertoire Bibliographique de la Philosophie.* Louvain: Institut Supérieur de Philosophie, 1949—. 4/yr.
An international, comprehensive, classified bibliography of books, articles, and reviews. Each issue is in two parts, one covering the history of philosophy and the other covering a variety of philosophical topics. Every fourth issue contains a book review index and a name index.

POETRY
There is no single bibliography of poetry criticism. See the following items as well as relevant period and author bibliographies.

(D106) *Anthology of Magazine Verse & Yearbook of American Poetry.*
Includes a selective list of books of poetry criticism.
(A1) *MLA International Bibliography.*
Poetry is a subheading under General Literature and Related Topics. IV. Themes and Types and under the various literary periods in Vols. I and II.
(B1) *Annual Bibliography of English Language and Literature.*
Poetry as a genre is included under Literary History and Criticism and under the various literary periods, Vol. 43, 1968—. Studies of meter and versification have, however, been listed in a separate section from Vol. 1 on.

POPULAR CULTURE
See also the sections on folklore, humor, science fiction, art and aesthetics, history, social sciences, and music in this chapter, as well as relevant sections in the *Bibliographie der deutschen Sprach- und Literaturwissenschaft* (C61) and the *Bibliographie der französischen Literaturwissenschaft* (C11). *Contemporary Literary Criticism* (B67) covers contemporary popular culture, Vol. 13—.

D311 *Abstracts of Popular Culture: A Quarterly Publication of International Popular Phenomena.* Bowling Green, Ohio: Popular Culture Press, 1975—. 4/yr. Temporarily suspended.

PROSE
D315 *Prose Studies.* Leicester: Univ. of Leicester, 1977—. 3/yr.
"Nineteenth-Century Non-Fictional Prose: A Bibliography of Work" lists books and articles on English and American writers and on literary aspects of nonfiction prose.

PSYCHOLOGY
See also *Language and Language Behavior Abstracts* (D253) and items under social sciences, below.
D321 *Literature and Psychology.* Teaneck, N.J.: Fairleigh Dickinson Univ., 1951—. 4/yr.
Carried an annual bibliography of articles through 1970 in Vols. 1–23, 1951–73, on literature and psychology.
D322 *Psychological Abstracts.* Washington, D.C.: American Psychological Assn., 1927—. 12/yr.
An international, comprehensive, classified bibliography of books, articles, dissertations, and some unpublished papers. All books and articles are abstracted. Author and subject indexes in each issue and cumulated semiannually. Relevant index headings: literature, poetry, prose, autobiography, and biography.
D323 *Contemporary Psychology.* Washington, D.C.: American Psychological Assn., 1956—. 12/yr.
Each issue publishes reviews of recent books in psychology; annual author and reviewer index.

REFERENCE BOOKS

Reference books having to do with individual authors and certain broader subjects are frequently reviewed in *The Year's Work in English Studies* (B2), *The Year's Work in Modern Language Studies* (C3), and *American Literary Scholarship* (B72).

D325 *Reference Services Review: A Quarterly Guide to the World of Reference*. Ann Arbor: Pierian, 1973—. 4/yr.

    "Reference Sources" in each issue is a selectively annotated list of new reference books in all subjects. Reviews of new reference books are indexed. The index supplements Shirley Smith, ed., *Reference Book Review Index 1970–1972* (Ann Arbor: Pierian, 1975) and M. and S. Balachandran, eds., *Reference Book Review Index 1973–1975* (Ann Arbor: Pierian, 1979).

D326 *American Reference Book Annual*. Littleton, Colo.: Libraries Unlimited, 1970—. Annual.

    A classified, selective bibliography of new reference books chiefly in English. The section for literature lists titles by form (such as bibliography, handbook, biography) and then by national literature. Author, subject, and title index.

D327 *American Notes and Queries*. Owingsville, Ky.: Erasmus, 1962—. 10/yr.

    "Recent Books" (originally "Recent Foreign Reference Books," Vol. 1–12) lists new titles with brief descriptive annotations.

D328 *Reference Book Review*. Columbia, S.C.: Reference Book Review, 1976—. 4/yr.

    About 100–150 recent reference books in most fields, except medicine, technology, and agriculture, are listed annually, with descriptive and evaluative annotations.

REGIONALISM (U.S.A.)

Except for the section in *Abstracts of English Studies* (B3) that covers regionalism in Great Britain and the U.S.A., only bibliographies for American regional studies are listed here. See also under black studies, ethnic studies, folklore, and history, above.

(B3) *Abstracts of English Studies*.

    See sections for regionalist studies of both English and American literature.

D331 *Western American Literature*. Logan, Utah: Western American Literature Assn., 1966—. 4/yr.

    The "Annual Bibliography of Studies in Western American Literature," 1965—, lists books and articles about Western writers, including Native Americans, and about Western literature in general.

D332 *Mississippi Quarterly: The Journal of Southern Culture*. Mississippi State: Mississippi State Univ., 1947—. 4/yr.

    "A Checklist of Scholarship on Southern Literature," 1968—, is an annual list of books and articles on Southern writers, arranged in five parts: colonial, antebellum (1860–65), postbellum, contemporary (1920—), and general.

The bibliographies for 1968–75 have been collected, cumulated, and supplemented: Jerry T. Williams, ed., *Southern Literature 1968–1975: A Checklist of Scholarship* (Boston: Hall, 1978).

D333 *Midamerica.* East Lansing, Mich.: Center for the Study of Midwestern Literature, 1973—. Annual.

"Annual Bibliography of Studies in Midwestern Literature" lists American books and articles on general literary topics and on individual writers.

D334 *The Great Lakes Review: A Journal of Midwest Culture.* Mt. Pleasant: Central Michigan Univ., 1974—. 2/yr.

(Published at Northeastern Illinois Univ., Chicago, 1974–78.)

An annual bibliography lists creative writing as well as studies of literary and related topics.

D335 *The North Carolina Historical Review.* Raleigh: North Carolina Division of Archives and History, 1924—. 4/yr.

"North Carolina Bibliography," 1933—, is an annual, classified bibliography of books and articles by North Carolinians or about North Carolina; among the categories are philosophy and literary studies and poetry, fiction, and other creative writing.

RHETORIC. See Composition and Rhetoric.

SCIENCE AND TECHNOLOGY

D341 *Clio: An Interdisciplinary Journal of Literature, History, and the Philosophy of History.* Fort Wayne: Indiana Univ.–Purdue Univ., 1971—. 3/yr.

"Relations of Literature and Science: A Bibliography of Scholarship," 1972— (Vol.4, 1974—), is an annual, international classified bibliography of books and articles, arranged under headings for general studies, antiquity and the Middle Ages, the Renaissance, and each of the succeeding centuries.

Continues an earlier bibliography, Fred A. Dudley, *The Relations of Literature and Science: A Selected Bibliography, 1930-1967* (Ann Arbor: University Microfilms, 1968), that cumulated coverage for 1951–67 in *Symposium: A Quarterly Journal of Modern Foreign Literatures* (Syracuse, N.Y.: Syracuse Univ. Press) and for 1939–50 in *Relations of Literature and Science: A Bibliography of Scholarship*, an annual bibliography mimeographed by the Modern Language Association.

(D83) *Yearbook of Comparative and General Literature.*

See the annual bibliographies for 1949–69 for occasional coverage of the relations between literature and science.

D342 *Isis: An International Review Devoted to the History of Science and Its Cultural Influences.* Washington, D.C.: History of Science Soc., 1913—. 5/yr.

"Critical Bibliography of the History of Science and Its Cultural Influences," 1913— (published as a supplement, Vol. 58, 1969—), is a classified, international, annual, and comprehensive bibliography of books and articles, with a separate book review index and name index for authors and subjects.

Cumulated: Magda Whitrow, *Isis Cumulative Bibliography: A Bibliography of the History of Science Formed from Isis Critical Bibliographies, 1–90, 1913–1965,* 3 Vols. (London: Mansell, 1971–77).

D343 *Technology and Culture: The International Quarterly of the Society for the History of Technology.* Chicago: Univ. of Chicago Press, 1961—. 4/yr.

Carries an annual, international, classified bibliography of books and articles, 1961— (Vol.4, 1964—), with items arranged by subject under broad chronological periods. Frequent, brief annotations. Author index; biennial subject index.

D344 *Bibliography of the History of Medicine.* Bethesda, Md.: U.S. National Library of Medicine, 1965—. Annual.

Comprehensive, classified, international bibliography of books and articles, for 1964—. Section 1 covers studies on individuals, arranged alphabetically by the subject's name (see, for example, Goethe, Rousseau, Shakespeare). Section 2 covers subjects (see, for example, Literature and Medicine). Author index.

D345 *Bulletin of the History of Medicine.* Baltimore: Johns Hopkins Univ. Press, 1933—. 4/yr.

"Bibliography of the History of Medicine in the United States and Canada," for 1939–65 (in Vols. 8–40, 1940–66), listed books and articles.

Cumulated: Genevieve Miller, *Bibliography of the History of Medicine of the United States and Canada, 1939–1960* (Baltimore: Johns Hopkins Univ. Press, 1964).

D346 *Bulletin Signalétique 522: Histoire des Sciences et des Techniques.* Paris: Centre National de la Recherche Scientifique, 1948—. 4/yr.

Quarterly, classified bibliography of international books and articles on the history of science and technology. Subject and author indexes in each issue and cumulated annually.

D347 *General Science Index.* New York: Wilson, 1978—. 10/yr.

An author and subject index to articles and reviews in about 90 English language science magazines. See, for example, headings for history and philosophy of science and for science and literature.

More comprehensive coverage is provided by *Applied Science and Technology Index* (New York: Wilson, 1958—) and *Biological and Agricultural Index* (New York: Wilson, 1964—) and their predecessor, *Industrial Arts Index* (New York: Wilson, 1913–57).

D348 *Index to Book Reviews in the Sciences.* Philadelphia: Inst. for Scientific Information, 1981—. 12/yr.

An author index to book reviews, with a key-word-in-title index to books reviewed.

D349 *Science Books and Films.* Washington, D.C.: American Assn. for the Advancement of Science, 1965—. 12/yr.

Each issue carries reviews of books and films on all aspects of science, medicine, and certain social sciences (psychology, sociology, anthropology, economics, and folklore). Annual author index for books and a corporate index for films.

D350 *Journal of American Culture.* Bowling Green, Ohio: Bowling Green State Univ., 1978—. 4/yr.

"Technology in American Culture: Recent Publications," 1980—, is a regular annotated list of mainly American books and articles.

SCIENCE FICTION

For indexes to current science fiction, as well as to other fiction, see D110–D116, above. See also *Contemporary Literary Criticism* (B67) as well as the general indexes, A6–A27.

D351   *Extrapolation: A Journal of Science Fiction and Fantasy.* Kent, Ohio: Kent State Univ. Press, 1959—. 2/yr.

"The Year's Scholarship in Science Fiction and Fantasy," 1972— (Vol. 17—, 1975—), lists books, articles, dissertations, and instructional visual media, mainly from the U.S.A., under four headings: General, Reference and Bibliography, Teaching and Visual Aids, and Authors. Each item is annotated.

Cumulated: Marshall B. Tymn and Roger C. Schlobin, eds., *The Year's Scholarship in Science Fiction and Fantasy, 1972–1975* (Kent, Ohio: Kent State Univ. Press, 1979).

Continues Thomas Clareson, ed., *Science Fiction Criticism: An Annotated Checklist* (Kent, Ohio: Kent State Univ. Press, 1972).

(A1)   *MLA International Bibliography.*

Studies of science fiction are listed under the Prose Fiction heading under General Literature and Related Topics. IV. Themes and Types in Vol. I, and under the twentieth-century sections of English and American literature.

(C11)   *Bibliographie der französischen Literaturwissenschaft.*

Science Fiction is a subsection under Généralités, Vol. 12—, 1974—. Only French language books and articles are listed.

D352   *The N.E.S.F.A. Index: Science Fiction Magazines and Original Anthologies.* Cambridge, Mass.: New England Science Fiction Writers, 1971—. Annual.

An author, title, and periodical/anthology index to creative writing, criticism, book reviews, and commentary on English language (including some translations) science fiction and fantasy writing.

Supplements: Erwin S. Strauss, *The MIT Science Fiction Society's Index to the S-F Magazines, 1951–1965* (Cambridge, Mass.: MIT Science Fiction Soc., 1965) and Donald B. Day, *Index to the Science Fiction Magazines, 1936–1950* (Portland, Ore.: Perri, 1952).

D353   *SFBRI: Science Fiction Book Review Index.* Bryan, Texas: SFBRI, 1970—. Annual.

An author list of science fiction, fantasy, and books of related interest, including reference books and criticism. Supplements the *Science Fiction Book Review Index, 1923–1973* (Detroit: Gale, 1975).

D354   *Science Fiction and Fantasy Book Review.* Vista, Calif.: Borgo, 1979—. 11/yr.

Attempts to review most of the yearly 1,000-1,500 English language science fiction and fantasy books.

D355   *Science Fiction Chronicle.* New York: Algol, 1979—. 12/yr.

Each issue includes a publisher list of new science fiction books.

(D116) *International Science Fiction Yearbook.*
Provides information about prizes, libraries and collections, magazines, film, radio, and television.

SCOTTISH STUDIES
See also items listed above under Celtic Studies and History.

D361 *Annual Bibliography of Scottish Literature.* Stirling: The Bibliothek, 1969—. Annual.
An international, classified bibliography of books, reviews, and articles for 1956—, arranged under headings for general studies, individual authors, and ballads and folk literature. Author and critic indexes. Carried as part of *The Bibliothek,* 1956–68.

D362 *Scottish Literary Journal: A Review of Studies in Scottish Languages and Literature.* Aberdeen: Assn. for Scottish Literary Studies, 1974—. 2/yr.
(Continues *Scottish Literary News,* 1970–74.)
"The Year's Work in Scottish Literary Studies," 1969—, is an annual (fall supplement) bibliographic essay reviewing selected items listed in the *Annual Bibliography of Scottish Literature.*
Includes an annual checklist of new creative writing in Scotland.

SOCIAL SCIENCES, SOCIOLOGY, ANTHROPOLOGY
D365 *Social Sciences Index.* New York: Wilson, 1974—. 4/yr.
(Formerly *Social Sciences and Humanities Index,* 1965–74, and *International Index,* 1916–65.)
An author and subject index to predominantly North American periodicals in the social and behavioral sciences, excluding history, which is covered in the *Humanities Index* (A8). See such headings as autobiography, literature and society, politics and literature, and psychological aspects of literature. Book reviews listed separately.

D366 *Social Sciences Citation Index.* Philadelphia: Inst. for Scientific Information, 1973—. 3/yr.
An author, citation, permuted title, and institution index to articles, correspondence, and notes in about 1,500 international periodicals in the social sciences, excluding history, which is covered in the *Arts and Humanities Citation Index* (A6).

D367 *Bulletin Signalétique 521: Sociologie, Ethnologie.* Paris: Centre National de la Recherche Scientifique, 1948—. 4/yr.
An international, comprehensive, classified bibliography of books and articles. See particularly the sections *Sociologie de l'art de la littérature* and *Sociologie de la communication et des mass media.* Subject and author indexes in each issue and cumulated annually.

D368 *Sociological Abstracts.* San Diego, Calif.: Sociological Abstracts, 1952—. 5/yr.
Classified, international, comprehensive bibliographical abstracts of articles in sociology. Categories include history, theory, and methodology of sociology; areas of sociological study (such as organizations, the family, political institutions, the arts); and more specialized studies (such as violence, feminism, Marxism, the sociology of knowledge). Author and subject index.

D369 *International Bibliography of Sociology.* Paris: UNESCO, 1952—. Annual. (Part of the *International Bibliography of the Social Sciences* series.)

   A classified, comprehensive, international list of books and articles in sociology. Subject and author indexes.

D370 *Contemporary Sociology.* Washington, D.C.: American Sociological Assn., 1972—. 6/yr.

   Reviews recent books in several categories such as aging, the arts, methods, organizations, social theory, etc. Multiple reviews of selected books and review articles are additional features. Annual author index of books reviewed.

D371 *Abstracts in Anthropology.* Farmingdale, N.Y.: Baywood, 1970—. 4/yr.

   International, classified bibliographical abstracts of articles. Author and subject indexes. Categories of special relevance to literary studies are arts (folklore, graphic arts, literature, music) and symbol systems (religion, ritual, and world view).

D372 *International Bibliography of Social and Cultural Anthropology.* Chicago: Aldine, 1955—. Annual. (Part of the *International Bibliography of the Social Sciences* series.)

   An international, comprehensive, and classified bibliography of books and articles on social and cultural anthropology; author and detailed subject indexes.

SPEECH COMMUNICATION

See also items listed under journalism and mass communication, linguistics and language, social sciences, and composition and rhetoric.

D375 *Southern Speech Communication Journal.* Knoxville, Tenn.: Southern Speech Assn., 1935—. 4/yr.

   "A Bibliography of Speech, Theatre, and Mass Communication in the South," 1954—, is an annual, classified bibliography of books, reviews, articles, and dissertations on public address, theater, speech education, and mass communication published in Southern journals or about people and conditions in the South.

D376 *Speech Communication Abstracts.* Pleasant Hill, Calif.: Theatre/Drama and Speech Information Center, 1975–80.

   (Titled *Theatre/Drama & Speech Index*, 1974. See D152.)

   An international, comprehensive abstracting service for articles, 1974–77. Author and subject index.

D377 *Bibliographic Annual in Speech Communication.* Falls Church, Va.: Speech Communication Assn., 1970–75. Annual.

   A classified, international, and comprehensive bibliography for 1969–74 of books, articles, dissertations, and theses in various areas of speech communication studies, mass communication, rhetoric, public address and oral interpretation, and theatrical craftsmanship.

   Previously carried in *Speech Monographs* (Falls Church, Va.: Speech Communication Assn., 1934–75). Theses listed for 1902–68, in Vols. 1–36, 1934–69; theses abstracted for 1945–68, in Vols. 13–36, 1946–69; and books, articles, and dissertations listed for 1950–68, in Vols. 18–36, 1951–69.

STYLE
See also items in sections on composition, art, linguistics, and literary genres.

D381 *Style*. Fayetteville: Univ. of Arkansas, 1967—. 4/yr.
Carries an annual, international, annotated bibliography, for 1966—, of books, articles, and dissertations on style in English and European literatures. Items are arranged under seven headings: Bibliographical Reviews; Theoretical Orientations; Rhythm and Sound; Imagery, Diction, and Figures of Speech; Syntax; Discourse and Rhetoric; and Language, Culture, Style.

TELEVISION AND RADIO. See Journalism and Mass Communication.

THEOLOGY AND RELIGION
See also bibliographies listed under philosophy, history, social sciences, and comparative literature, and under the literary periods and national literatures in Chapters iii and iv.

D385 *Religion Index One: Periodicals*. Chicago: American Theological Library Assn., 1949—. 4/yr., with annual cumulation.
(Formerly *Index to Religious Periodicals*, 1949–77.)
An author and subject index, with abstracts, to predominantly English language periodicals. Book review index. Broad coverage of literary and humanities subjects, as well as of religious and theological issues. Companion to:

D386 *Religion Index Two: Multi-Author Works*. Chicago: American Theological Library Assn., 1978—. Annual.
An author and subject index to international collective volumes on religion, 1976—; subject terms are identical with *Religion Index One*.

D387 *Christianity and Literature*. Adrian, Mich.: Adrian College, 1952—. 4/yr.
(Formerly *Conference on Christianity in Literature Newsletter*.)
Carries an annual, annotated author list of articles on literature and Christianity.

D388 *Religious and Theological Abstracts*. Myerstown, Pa.: Religious and Theological Abstracts, 1958—. 4/yr.
An international, classified bibliography of periodical articles, with abstracts and annual, cumulated author, subject, and scripture indexes. The abstracts are arranged in five main parts, each with subsections: biblical, theological, historical, practical (such as ministry, pastoral care, church administration), and sociological subjects.

D389 *International Bibliography of the History of Religions/Bibliographie Internationale de l'Histoire des Religions*. Leiden: Brill, 1954—. Annual.
An international, comprehensive, classified bibliography of books and articles on religion in general and on specific religions, prehistoric, ancient, and modern. Author index.

D390 *Elenchus Bibliographicus Biblicus*. Rome: Biblical Inst., 1920—. Annual.
An international, comprehensive, and classified bibliography of books, reviews, articles, and dissertations on biblical (but not necessar-

ily Christian) matters. Author and subject indexes. Editorial matter, including subject headings, in Latin.

D391   *Bulletin Signalétique 527: Sciences Religieuses.* Paris: Centre National de la Recherche Scientifique, 1948—. 4/yr.

An international, classified bibliography of articles from about 1,000 journals on religion in general, the ancient religions, Judaism, and Christianity and the Bible. Subject and author indexes in each issue and cumulated annually.

D392   *Catholic Periodical and Literature Index.* Haverford, Pa.: Catholic Library Assn., 1930—. 6/yr.

An author, title, and subject index to periodical articles and books by, or of interest to, Catholics. Covers about 120 periodicals and fifty books in each issue. Book review index.

D393   *New Testament Abstracts: A Record of Current Literature.* Cambridge, Mass.: Weston School of Theology, 1956—. 3/yr.

International, comprehensive, classified list of abstracts of books and articles. Annual indexes for biblical texts, book reviews, authors of articles, and authors and titles of books.

(C97)   *Quarterly Check-List of Oriental Studies.*

Superseded the *Quarterly Check-List of Biblical Studies* (Darien, Conn.: American Bibliographical Service, 1958–73). Coverage provided for 1958–78.

WOMEN'S STUDIES

See also bibliographies listed under history, psychology, and social sciences.

D401   *Women & Literature: A Journal of Women Writers and Literary Treatment of Women.* New York: Holmes and Meier, 1972—. Annual.

(Formerly *The Mary Wollstonecraft Newsletter,* 1972–74; published 4/yr., 1972-79.)

"Bibliography of Literature in English by and about Women," Vols. 3–7, 1975–79, was an annual, classified, international bibliography of books, reviews, and articles, for 1972–78, on women writers and on the treatment of women in literature. Occasional brief annotations.

D402   *Women Studies Abstracts.* Rush, N.Y.: Rush, 1972—. 4/yr.

A classified list of articles, chiefly from U.S. journals, with abstracts provided for about 25% of the citations.

Subject index in each issue. Categories include sex roles, family, religion, mental and physical health, literature and art, women's liberation movement.

D403   *Signs: A Journal for Women in Culture and Society.* Chicago: Univ. of Chicago Press, 1965—. 4/yr.

The "New Scholarship" section regularly publishes bibliographic essays on a variety of subjects including literary criticism.

Chapter Six.   Authors

   This chapter includes only books and journals that regularly carry a checklist of criticism, a review of current scholarship, or enough book reviews and news to be a reliable source of up-to-date information about scholarly activities on an author. It excludes the many author journals that publish useful bibliographies irregularly. The most complete list of serial publications concerned with individual authors is Margaret Patterson's *Author Newsletters and Journals* (Detroit: Gale, 1979), but not all the items listed carry bibliographies. Despite the happy proliferation of author journals and bibliographies, anyone looking for author bibliographies will probably still have to use a number of sources, such as the standard literary bibliographies, relevant period, subject, and genre bibliographies, and the *Bibliographic Index* (D19).
   An author bibliography, especially one published in an author journal that also carries book reviews and news, has a number of virtues not found in a more general and comprehensive bibliography. It can be at once broad and specialized in its coverage of the subject author; it can be very current (even to the point of listing forthcoming publications and suggestions for further research); and it can provide information about archives, collections, meetings, and other matters of interest to scholars and enthusiasts. The breadth comes from being able to cite not only books, articles, and dissertations—all fairly easily found—but also newspaper articles, media presentations and materials, unpublished papers, forthcoming books and articles, mentions of the author in works on other subjects, and other out-of-the-way items. The specialization comes from having bibliographers familiar enough with the subject to be able to provide not only descriptive annotations but also critical or evaluative annotations and bibliographic essays. Occasionally, as with the *Keats-Shelley Journal* and the *Stendhal Club* bibliographies, there can be thorough subject indexing for the bibliography. Of course, author bibliographies can be impressionistic, provincial, unsympathetic to new approaches and interpretations, and overloaded with trivia, but these failings can coexist with the virtues of breadth, specialization, and currentness.
   Bibliographies are listed alphabetically by subject authors.

ANDERSEN
   E1 *Anderseniana.* Copenhagen: Universitetsbiblioteket, 1933—. Annual.
      Has carried a review of research for 1960— (in Vol. 1961—).

APOLLINAIRE
   (C25) *La Revue des Lettres Modernes.*
      Guillaume Apollinaire is a subseries, 1962—.

ARNOLD
E4   *The Arnoldian.* Annapolis, Md: U.S. Naval Academy, 1974—. 3/yr.
Annual bibliographic essay appears in the third issue.

BALZAC
E7   *L'Année Balzacienne.* Paris: Garnier, 1960—. Annual.
(Supersedes *Études Balzacienne,* 1951–60, and *Le Courrier Balzacien,* 1948–50.)
Annual bibliography, 1960—, of books (including editions), articles, and dissertations.

BARBEY D'AUREVILLY
(C25)   *La Revue des Lettres Modernes.*
Barbey d'Aurevilly is a subseries, 1966—.

BAUDELAIRE
E10   *Bulletin Baudelairien.* Nashville: Vanderbilt Univ., 1965—. 2/yr.
An annual bibliography in the first issue lists books, articles, dissertations, and theses.

BECKETT
(C25)   *La Revue des Lettres Modernes.*
Samuel Beckett is a subseries.

HJALMAR BERGMAN
E13   *Hjalmar Bergman Samfundet-Årsbok.* Stockholm: Hjalmar Bergman Samfundet, 1959—. Annual.
"Hjalmar Bergman Bibliografi," an international list of works by and about Bergman, appears biennially, 1959–69, and triennially, 1970—.

BERNANOS
(C25)   *La Revue des Lettres Modernes.*
Études Bernanos is a subseries, 1960—.

BLAKE
See also these two important annotated bibliographies: *The Eighteenth Century: A Current Bibliography* (B41) and *The Romantic Movement: A Critical and Selective Bibliography* (B51).

E16   *Blake: An Illustrated Quarterly.* Albuquerque: Univ. of New Mexico, 1967—. 4/yr.
(Formerly *Blake Newsletter: An Illustrated Quarterly,* Vol.1–10.)
"A Checklist of Recent Blake Scholarship" is an annual, international, and comprehensive list of bibliographies (including exhibition catalogs), editions (including facsimiles), critical studies (books, articles, and dissertations), and reviews.

BOCCACCIO
E19   *Studi sul Boccaccio.* Florence: Sansoni, 1963—. Annual.
An international and comprehensive list of books, articles, and translations, with the first three volumes gathering studies done since 1938. Editorial matter in Italian.

BROWNING
   E22 *Studies in Browning and His Circle: A Journal of Criticism, History,
        and Bibliography.* Waco, Texas: Armstrong Browning Library, 1973—.
        2/yr.
        (Continues *Browning Newsletter*, 1968–72.)
        "Checklist of Publications," in each issue starting in the *Browning
        Newsletter*, No. 1, 1968, is an international and comprehensive list of
        bibliographical aids, books, reviews, articles, and dissertations. Each
        issue also lists research in progress (including dissertations), perfor-
        mances, symposia, exhibits, and desiderata.
   E25 *Browning Institute Studies.* New York: Browning Inst., 1973—. Annual.
        "Robert and Elizabeth Barrett Browning: An Annotated Bibliogra-
        phy," for 1971—, is a comprehensive, international, and annotated list of
        editions, reference and bibliographical books, and of books, reviews, ar-
        ticles, dissertations, and exhibitions. Index of critics, book reviewers,
        and titles of the Brownings' works.

BYRON
   (B52) *Keats-Shelley Journal.*
          Lists studies on Byron and his circle.

CAMUS
   (C25) *La Revue des Lettres Modernes.*
          Albert Camus is a subseries, 1961—.

CARLYLE
   E28 *The Carlyle Newsletter.** Edinburgh: Univ. of Edinburgh; Easton,
        Penn.: Lafayette College, 1979—. Annual.
        Carries a bibliography of books and articles.

CÉLINE
   (C25) *La Revue des Lettres Modernes.*
          L.-F. Céline is a subseries, 1974—.

CERVANTES
   E31 *Anales Cervantinos.* Madrid: Consejo Superior de Investigaciones Cien-
        tíficas, 1951—. Annual.
        "Bibliografia Cervantina" is an international and classified bibliogra-
        phy of books, reviews, and articles, with annotations in Spanish. Items
        arranged under sections for bibliographies, general studies, biography,
        Don Quixote, and the other works.

CHATEAUBRIAND
   E34 *Société Chateaubriand: Bulletin.* La Vallée-aux-Loups: Société
        Chateaubriand, 1956—. Annual.
        Carries an international list of books and articles for 1958—.

CHAUCER
   Both the *MLAIB* (A1) and *YWES* (B2) devote a separate section to Chaucer
   studies.

E37 *Studies in the Age of Chaucer.* Norman, Okla.: New Chaucer Soc.,
     1979—. Annual.
     "An Annotated Chaucer Bibliography," for 1975—, is an interna-
     tional, classified, annotated bibliography of books, reviews, articles, and
     dissertations.
E40 *The Chaucer Review: A Journal of Medieval Studies and Literary Criti-
     cism.* University Park: Pennsylvania State Univ. Press, 1966—. 4/yr.
     "Chaucer Research Report" is an annual list of books (including edi-
     tions), articles, and dissertations, chiefly by North Americans. Formerly
     published in mimeograph form by the MLA's Chaucer Group, 1941–
     65.
     A list of works in progress, projects completed but unpublished, and
     desiderata is carried here and in *Neuphilologische Mitteilungen* (B20).

CLAUDEL
(C25) *La Revue des Lettres Modernes.*
       Paul Claudel is a subseries, 1964—.

CLEMENS (Mark Twain)
E43 *American Literary Realism.* Arlington: Univ. of Texas, Arlington, 1967—.
     4/yr.
     Annual, international, and comprehensive list of books, articles, and
     dissertations, 1977—.
     This updates Thomas Asa Tenney, *Mark Twain: A Reference Guide*
     (Boston: Hall, 1977).
     See also the bibliographies listed under Regionalism in Chapter v.

COCTEAU
E46 *Cahiers Jean Cocteau.* Paris: Gallimard, 1969—. 4/yr.
     "Bibliographie" is an annual, selective list of editions (including trans-
     lations) and of French books and articles.
(C25) *La Revue des Lettres Modernes.*
       Jean Cocteau is a subseries, 1970—.

COLERIDGE
(E290) *The Wordsworth Circle.*
        "Coleridge Scholarship: An Annual Register," for 1971—, appears in
        the summer issue, Vol. 3—, 1972—, and lists books, reviews, articles,
        and dissertations.

COLETTE
E49 *Cahiers Colette.* Paris: Flammarion, 1977—. Frequency not known.
     "Bibliographie" in each issue.

CONRAD
E52 *Conradiana.* Lubbock: Texas Tech Univ., 1968—. 3/yr.
     "Conrad Bibliography: A Continuing Checklist" is an annual, interna-
     tional list of books (including editions), reviews, articles, and disserta-
     tions, 1967—.

CRANE
    E55 *Stephen Crane Newsletter*. Columbia, S.C., 1966–70. 4/yr.
        "Quarterly Checklist" of criticism appeared in each issue, along with
        reviews of books, films, and plays.
    E56 *Thoth*. Syracuse, N.Y.: Syracuse Univ., 1959—. 3/yr.
        "Stephen Crane Bibliography," 1963–75, was an annual list of critical
        and biographical studies (books and articles) and of editions and manu-
        scripts. The lists for 1963–69, with additional items, were cumulated
        and included in "A Bibliography of Stephen Crane Scholarship: 1893–
        1969," published as a special supplement in *Thoth*, 10 (1970), but bound
        in Vol. 11 (1971).
        This continues Robert N. Hudspeth, "A Bibliography of Stephen
        Crane Scholarship: 1893–1962," *Thoth*, 4 (1963), 31–58.

DANTE
    E59 *Dante Studies*. Albany: Dante Soc. of America, 1882—. Annual.
        "American Dante Bibliography," 1953—, is an annotated list of books,
        reviews, articles, and dissertations published in North America.
    E60 *Studi Danteschi*. Florence: Sansoni, 1920—. Annual.
        (Supersedes *Bullettino della Società Dantesca Italiana* [Florence:
        Società Dantesca Italiana, 1890–1921].)
        Carries a bibliography of books and articles, chiefly by Italian scholars
        and with annotations in Italian, Vol. 13—, 1928—. The *Bullettino* car-
        ried an annual bibliography of Dante criticism, 1890—.
    E61 *L'Alighieri: Rassegna Bibliografica Dantesca.** Rome: Rassegna Bib-
        liografica Dantesca, 1960—. 2/yr.
        Carries an annual bibliography of Italian Dante studies.

DEFOE
    (B43) *The Scriblerian and the Kit-Cats*.
        Coverage of Defoe begins in 1980.

DICKENS
    E65 *Dickens Studies Newsletter*. Louisville: Dickens Soc., 1970—. 4/yr.
        "The Dickens Checklist" in each issue is a comprehensive, interna-
        tional list of editions, studies (books, reviews, articles, and disserta-
        tions), and miscellaneous items (for example, audiovisual programs,
        screenplays, and teaching aids).
    E66 *The Dickensian*. London: Dickens Fellowship, 1905—. 3/yr.
        Annual bibliographic essay, "Year's Work in Dickens Studies," 1968—,
        lists books and surveys the year's periodical literature.

DICKINSON
    E69 *Dickinson Studies*. Brentwood, Md: Higginson, 1968—. 2/yr.
        (Titled *Emily Dickinson Bulletin*, 1968–78.)
        "Emily Dickinson Annual Bibliography" lists books and articles.

DONNE
    (B33) *Seventeenth-Century News*.
        Each issue carries abstracts of recent, international articles on Donne
        and other 17th-century English and American writers.

DOSTOEVSKY

E72   *International Dostoevsky Society Bulletin.* Washington, D.C.: International Dostoevsky Soc., 1971—. Annual.

"Current Bibliography," 1971—, is an international and comprehensive list of books, articles, and dissertations. The *IDS Bulletin* also publishes abstracts of conference papers.

DOYLE

E75   *Baker Street Journal: An Irregular Quarterly.* New York: Fordham Univ. Press, 1946—. 4/yr.

"Baker Street Inventory" in each issue lists new books and articles about, and new periodicals devoted to, Doyle.

DREISER

E78   *Dreiser Newsletter.* Terre Haute: Indiana State Univ., 1970—. 2/yr.

Each fall issue carries an annotated list of editions and studies (books, articles, and dissertations).

DRYDEN

(B43)   *The Scriblerian and the Kit-Cats.*

Abstracts current articles on Dryden and other writers of the period.

(B33)   *Seventeenth-Century News.*

Each issue lists abstracts of recent international articles on Dryden and other 17th-century English and American writers.

EICHENDORFF

E81   *Aurora: Jahrbuch der Eichendorff-Gesellschaft.* Würzburg: Eichendorff-Gesellschaft, 1931—. Annual.

"Eichendorff Bibliographie" lists books and articles, editions, and musical settings of Eichendorff's works.

T. S. ELIOT

Eliot is listed in the English literature sections of the *MLA International Bibliography* (A1) and *The Year's Work in English Studies* (B2).

E84   *Yeats Eliot Review.* Edmonton: Univ. of Alberta, 1974—. 2/yr.
(Titled *T. S. Eliot Review,* 1974–78.)

"Bibliographical Update" in each issue is an international and comprehensive list of books, articles, and dissertations.

EMERSON

E87   *American Transcendental Quarterly.* Kingston: Univ. of Rhode Island, 1969—. 4/yr.
(Nos. 1–32 published at Hartford, Conn.)

"Current Bibliography on Ralph Waldo Emerson," 1972—, is an annual list of books, articles, and dissertations (including some in progress).

The same bibliography was previously carried for 1955–72 in *ESQ: Journal of the American Renaissance* (Pullman: Washington State Univ.).

ERASMUS
E90 *Erasmus in English.* Toronto: Univ. of Toronto Press, 1970—. Irregular.
"Recent Publications" in each issue lists international books and articles.

FIELDING
(B43) *The Scriblerian and the Kit-Cats.*
Coverage of Fielding studies begins in 1980.

FITZGERALD
E93 *Fitzgerald/Hemingway Annual.* Detroit: Gale, 1970—. Annual. (Publisher varies.)
(Continues *Fitzgerald Newsletter*, 1958–68.)
Carries an international and comprehensive list of books, articles, and newspaper stories, 1957—. Each volume also notes addenda to the Bruccoli bibliography: Matthew J. Bruccoli, *F. Scott Fitzgerald: A Descriptive Bibliography* (Pittsburgh: Univ. of Pittsburgh Press, 1972).

FLAUBERT
E96 *Les Amis de Flaubert.* Rouen: Les Amis de Flaubert, 1951—. 2/yr.
"Bibliographie," for 1951—, is an annual, international list of books and articles.

GIDE
(C25) *La Revue des Lettres Modernes.*
Andre Gide is a subseries, 1970—.

GIONO
(C25) *La Revue des Lettres Modernes.*
Jean Giono is a subseries, 1973—.

GISSING
E99 *Gissing Newsletter.* Dorking: Gissing Newsletter, 1965—. 4/yr.
"Recent Publications" in each issue lists reprints and criticism (books, articles, newspaper stories).

GOETHE
Both the *Bibliographie der deutschen Sprach- und Literaturwissenschaft* (C61) and *Germanistik* (C62) devote separate sections to Goethe and *Goethezeit*.

E102 *Goethe-Jahrbuch.* Weimar: Böhlaus, 1936—. Annual.
"Goethe-Bibliographie," 1951—, is an international and comprehensive list of primary materials, books, and articles. Critic index.

GRILLPARZER
E105 *Grillparzer Forum Forchtenstein.* Vienna: Grillparzer-Forum, 1965—. Annual.
"Grillparzer Bibliographie" is an annual, international list of books, articles, and dissertations.

HARDY

E108   *Thomas Hardy Yearbook*. Guernsey: Toucan, 1970—. Annual.
  "Thomas Hardy: A Bibliography" in each annual issue lists international books, articles, and dissertations.

HAUPTMANN

E111   *Schlesien: Arts, Science, Folklore*. Nuremberg: Nürnberg Presse, 1956—. 4/yr.
  "Gerhart-Hauptmann-Literatur," a biennial bibliographic essay on Hauptmann studies, covers international books and articles. In German.

HAWTHORNE

E114   *Nathaniel Hawthorne Journal*. Detroit: Gale 1971—. Annual.
  "Checklist" provides comprehensive and international coverage of editions, translations, and critical and bibliographical studies (books, articles, dissertations), 1970—.

HAZLITT

(B52)   *Keats-Shelley Journal*.
  Annual, comprehensive, and international bibliography of books and articles. Hazlitt items were listed in the Keats section of the bibliography until Vol. 24, 1977 (for year 1975), at which point they were put into a separate section on Hazlitt and Hunt.

HEBBEL

E117   *Hebbel-Jahrbuch*. Heide in Holstein: Westholsteinische Verlagaustalt Boyens, 1939—. Annual.
  "Literaturbericht" is a bibliographic essay in German discussing mainly German books, articles, and dissertations.

HEINE

E120   *Heine-Jahrbuch*. Hamburg: Hoffman und Campe, 1962—. Annual.
  "Heine Literatur [year] mit Nachträgen" is an international list of books, reviews, articles, and mentions of Heine in works on other subjects.

HEMINGWAY

(E93)   *Fitzgerald/Hemingway Annual*.
  "Checklist," 1974—, covers books, reviews, articles, newspaper stories, and primary materials.

HESSE

E123   *Hermann-Hesse Literatur*. Hannau: Hermann-Hesse Literatur, 1973—. Annual.
  An international list of books, articles, and dissertations.
  Updates Martin Pfeifer, *Hermann-Hesse-Bibliographie. Primär- und Sekundarschriftum in Auswahl* (Berlin: Schmidt, 1973).

HÖLDERLIN
  E126 *Hölderlin-Jahrbuch*. Tübingen: Friedrich-Hölderlin Gesellschaft, 1947—. Annual.
     (Titled *Iduna: Jahrbuch der Hölderlin-Gesellschaft*, 1944–46.)
     "Hölderlin Bibliographie" is an irregular, international, classified bibliography of editions, translations, and critical books, articles, and dissertations. Years 1966–70 in the 1973–74 vol.; years 1971–73 in vols. for 1975–77.

HOFMANNSTHAL
  E129 *Hofmannsthal Blätter*. Frankfurt am Main: Hugo von Hofmannsthal-Gesellschaft, 1968—. Annual.
     Each volume carries an international and comprehensive list of Hofmannsthal texts and letters and of books, articles, and dissertations about him.

HOPKINS
  E132 *The Hopkins Quarterly*. Waterloo, Ont.: Wilfrid Laurier Univ., 1974—. 4/yr.
     Carries an annual comprehensive and international bibliography. Includes excerpts from and evaluations of books and articles.
  E135 *Hopkins Research Bulletin*. Enfield: Hopkins Soc., 1970–76.
     Published an annual, international list of books, reviews, articles, dissertations, theses, and newspaper items.

HUNT
  (B52) *Keats-Shelley Journal*.
     A separate section of the bibliography is devoted to Hunt, 1952—.

IBSEN
  E138 *Ibsenårbok*. Oslo: Universitetsforlaget, 1952—. Biennial.
     "Ibsen-bibliografi," for 1953—, is an international list of books and articles.

JACOB
  (C25) *La Revue des Lettres Modernes*.
     Max Jacob is a subseries, 1972—.

JAMES
  E141 *Henry James Review*.* Baton Rouge: Louisiana State Univ. Press, 1979—. 3/yr.
     Carries an annual review of James criticism.

JOHNSON
  E144 *Johnsonian News Letter*. New York: Columbia Univ., 1940—. 4/yr.
     Most issues carry annotated announcements of new books on Johnson and 18th-century English literature; recent articles are cited occasionally.

JONSON
  (B33) *Seventeenth-Century News*.
     Each issue carries abstracts of recent, international articles.

JOYCE

E147   *James Joyce Quarterly*. Tulsa: Univ. of Tulsa, 1963—. 4/yr.
"Supplemental JJ Checklist" is an annual, comprehensive, and international bibliography of editions (especially translations), studies (books, reviews, articles), theatrical productions, musical settings, records, and miscellany.

KEATS

(B52)   *Keats-Shelley Journal: Keats, Shelley, Byron, Hunt and Their Circles*.
Carries an annual, comprehensive, international bibliography of Keats studies.

LARBAUD

E153   *Cahiers des Amis de Valéry Larbaud*. Vichy: Association des Amis de Valéry Larbaud, 1970—. Annual.
"Bibliographie Larbaudienne," an international list of books and articles about Larbaud, also records sales and donations of manuscript materials.

LAWRENCE

E156   *D. H. Lawrence Review*. Fayetteville: Univ. of Arkansas, 1968—. 3/yr.
"The Checklist of D. H. Lawrence Criticism and Scholarship," in the spring issue, is an international and comprehensive list of books, articles, and dissertations.

G. E. LESSING

E159   *Lessing Yearbook*. Munich: Hueber, 1969—. Annual.
Each annual volume contains extensive reviews of books on Lessing and 18th-century German literature.

C. S. LEWIS

E162   *Mythlore*. Whittier, Calif.: Mythopoeic Soc., 1969—. 4/yr.
"The Inklings Bibliography," in each issue, lists books, articles, and conference papers on Lewis, Tolkien, and Charles Williams. First appeared in issue No. 12, 1976 (also numbered Vol. 3, No. 4).

LONDON

E165   *Jack London Newsletter*. Carbondale: Southern Illinois Univ., 1967—. 3/yr.
"WLT[2]: Supplement," in every issue, Vol. 6, No. 4—, lists translations, new editions, and studies (books and articles).
Supplements: H. C. Woodbridge, John London, and G. H. Tweeney, eds., *Jack London: A Bibliography* (Georgetown, Calif.: Talisman, 1966).

LUTHER

E168   *Luther Jahrbuch*. Göttingen: Vandenhoeck and Ruprecht, 1919—. Annual. (Suspended 1942–56.)
"Lutherbibliographie [year]" is an annual, international, classified, and comprehensive bibliography, for 1940—, of books and articles on Luther

and related aspects of the Reformation, the history of books and printing, and German language and culture. Author and selective title index.

MALRAUX
(C25) *La Revue des Lettres Modernes.*
André Malraux is a subseries, 1971—.

MARTÍ
E171 *Anuario Martiano.* * Havana: Biblioteca Nacional José Martí, Consejo
National de Cultura, 1969—. Annual.
"Bibliografía martiana" is a bibliography of Martí studies.

MAUPASSANT
(E96) *Les Amis de Flaubert.*
Carries an annual, international bibliography of books and articles,
1960—.

MAURIAC
(C25) *La Revue des Lettres Modernes.*
François Mauriac is a subseries, 1974—.

MENCKEN
E174 *Menckeniana: A Quarterly Review.* Baltimore: Enoch Pratt Free Library, 1962—. 4/yr.
Nearly every issue lists primary items and secondary studies (books,
articles, and newspaper stories).

MILL
E177 *Mill News Letter.* Toronto: Univ. of Toronto, 1965—. 2/yr.
Each issue lists books and articles about Mill and related subjects.

MILTON
A separate chapter has been devoted to Milton in *The Year's Work in English
Studies* (B2), 1971—.

E180 *Milton Quarterly.* Athens: Ohio Univ., 1967—. 4/yr.
(Titled *Milton Newsletter*, Vol. 1–3, 1967–69.)
Each issue carries abstracts of about ten recent articles or papers.
(B33) *Seventeenth-Century News.*
Each issue carries abstracts of recent articles and dissertations about
Milton and other 17th-century English and American writers.

MARIANNE MOORE
E183 *Marianne Moore Newsletter.* Philadelphia: Rosenbach Foundation,
1977—. 2/yr.
Each issue lists newly discovered works by Moore, translations, and
critical studies (books, articles, and works in progress).

MUSIL
E186 *Musil-Forum.* * Saarbrucken: Internationale Robert-Musilgesellschaft,
1975—. Annual.

"Jahresbibliographie [year]" is an international list of editions and translations and of books and articles about Musil.

NABOKOV

E189 *The Vladimir Nabokov Research Newsletter.* Lawrence: Univ. of Kansas, 1979—. 2/yr.

Each issue carries a bibliography of recent books, articles, dissertations, and primary works, provides abstracts of recent dissertations, and lists work in progress.

NEWMAN

E192 *Newman Studies.** Nuremberg: Glock und Lutz, 1948—. Irregular.

"Newman-Bibliographe" is a comprehensive, international list of new editions and translations and of books and articles.

NIN

E195 *Under the Sign of Pisces: Anaïs Nin and Her Circle.* Columbus, Ohio: University Libraries, 1970—. 4/yr.

Each issue lists critical studies (books and articles), works by Nin, related books, articles, and other media, and news and notes of interest to collectors and scholars.

O'CASEY

E198 *The Sean O'Casey Review.* Holbrook, N.Y.: O'Casey Studies, 1974—. 2/yr.

An annual, international list of books and articles on O'Casey is carried in the fall issue.

O'NEILL

E201 *Eugene O'Neill Newsletter.* Boston: Suffolk Univ., 1977—. 3/yr.

Each issue lists abstracts or summaries of articles, papers, and dissertations.

PÉREZ GALDÓS

E204 *Anales Galdósianos.* Austin, Tex.: Asociación Internacional de Galdósianos, 1966—. Annual.

Carries an annual, international, classified bibliography of books, articles, dissertations, and conferences on Pérez Galdós, his works, and his social and cultural context.

POE

E207 *Poe Studies.* Pullman: Washington State Univ., 1968—. 2/yr.

(Formerly *Poe Newsletter,* 1968–69.)

"Current Poe Bibliography" is a comprehensive and international list of books, articles, dissertations, and editions. Publication is irregular, but the bibliography seems to appear about every 1½ years. Supplemented by "Fugitive Poe References" and "Current Poe Activities," both irregular. Preceded by checklists for 1962–66 in *Emerson Society Quarterly,* No. 38 (1965), pp. 144–47, and No. 47 (1967), pp. 84–86.

POPE
(B43) *The Scriblerian and the Kit-Cats.*
Each issue carries abstracts of articles on Pope and contemporary figures.

PROUST
E210 *Proust Research Association Newsletter.* Lawrence Kan.: Proust Research Assn., 1969—. 2/yr.
Each issue lists editions, books, articles, dissertations, works in progress, and selected abstracts of papers and forthcoming books.
E213 *Bulletin d'Informations Proustiennes.* Paris: Presses de l'Ecole Normale Supérieure, 1975—. 2/yr.
"Les Activités Proustiennes" in each issue lists new international studies, works in progress, and miscellaneous news.

PYNCHON
E216 *Pynchon Notes: A Newsletter.* Middletown, Conn.: Wesleyan Univ., 1979—. 2/yr.
Each issue contains a "News" section that lists books, articles, and forthcoming meetings and projects. Each issue also contains an international bibliography of books, reviews, articles, and dissertations.

RAABE
E219 *Jahrbuch der Raabe-Gesellschaft.* Brunswick: Waisenhaus, 1960—. Annual.
(Continues *Raabe-Jahrbuch*, 1950–59.)
Carries an international list of books, articles, and dissertations.

RACINE
E222 *Cahiers Raciniens.* Paris: Société Racinienne, 1957—. 2/yr.
Provides an annual international list, in the second issue, of editions, books, and articles.

RICHARDSON
(B43) *The Scriblerian and the Kit-Cats.*
Coverage of Richardson studies begins in 1980.

RIMBAUD
(C25) *La Revue des Lettres Modernes.*
Arthur Rimbaud is a subseries, 1972—.

ROUSSEAU
E225 *Annales de la Société Jean-Jacques Rousseau.* Geneva: Jullien, 1905—. Irregular.
Carries an international, comprehensive, classified bibliography, for 1904—, in each volume. See both "Bibliographie" and "Chronique."

SCHNITZLER
E228 *Modern Austrian Literature: Journal of the International Arthur Schnitzler Research Association.* Riverside, Calif.: International Arthur Schnitzler Research Assn., 1961—. 4/yr.

"Arthur Schnitzler Bibliography" is an annual comprehensive, international list, with occasional brief annotations in English, of primary and secondary literature (books, articles, and dissertations), translations, and research in progress.

SHAKESPEARE

The two major Shakespeare bibliographies are published in *Shakespeare Quarterly* and *Shakespeare-Jahrbuch;* each lists about 1,400 items and each is classified, international, comprehensive, and well indexed. "Shakespeare: Annotated World Bibliography," in *SQ*, is slightly more current than the other and, a significant feature, most entries are annotated. But the "Shakespeare-Bibliographie" in *Shakespeare-Jahrbuch* has about ten percent more entries. These two should be supplemented by the evaluative bibliographic essays in *Shakespeare Survey* and *The Year's Work in English Studies* (B2) and by the extensive bibliography on the Renaissance context in *Shakespearean Research and Opportunites* (B32).

E231   *Shakespeare Quarterly.* Washington, D.C.: Folger Shakespeare Library, 1950—. 4/yr.
(Supersedes *Shakespeare Association Bulletin.* New York: Shakespeare Assn. of America, 1924–49.)
"Shakespeare: Annotated World Bibliography" appears annually in the fall issue and is an international, comprehensive, and classified list of books, reviews, articles, dissertations, selected papers, reprints, productions, and reviews of productions. Most items are given a brief descriptive annotation; one section covers general studies (with subdivisions for biography, milieu studies, paleography, etc.), and the other covers individual plays. Subject and name indexes. Coverage has been continuous, and increasingly comprehensive, for 1924—.

E232   *Shakespeare-Jahrbuch.* Weimar: Böhlaus, 1965—. Annual.
(Continues the numbering of the original *Shakespeare-Jahrbuch.*)
"Shakespeare-Bibliographie" is an international, comprehensive, classified bibliography of editions and translations, books, reviews, articles, and dissertations. Critic index. Carried in *Deutsche Shakespeare-Gesellschaft West Jahrbuch* in 1964–66.

(A1)   *MLA International Bibliography.*
Coverage is comparable to that in *Shakespeare Quarterly.*

(B1)   *Annual Bibliography of English Language and Literature.*
Coverage is comparable to that in *Shakespeare Quarterly.*

(B2)   *The Year's Work in English Studies.*
A separate chapter is devoted to Shakespeare studies.

E233   *Shakespeare Newsletter.* Coral Gables, Fla.: Univ. of Miami, 1951—. 6/yr. (Place and publisher have varied.)
Each issue includes abstracts of dissertations and of about five to ten articles.

(B32)   *Shakespearean Research and Opportunities.*
Annual author list of works in progress by North American critics (books, editions, articles, and dissertations). Also publishes an annual, comprehensive, international, and annotated bibliography on a great variety of Renaissance intellectual issues.

E234 *Shakespeare Survey.* Cambridge: Cambridge Univ. Press, 1948—. Annual.

"The Year's Contributions to Shakespearian Study," 1948—, is a selective bibliographic essay, with chapters on critical studies, Shakespeare's life, times, and stage, and textual studies. Critic index.

E235 *Deutsche Shakespeare-Gesellschaft West Jahrbuch.* Heidelburg: Quelle & Meyer, 1964—. Annual.

Carries a selective, classified list of editions and books, reviews, and articles written in German, published in Germany, or about Shakespeare and Germany (including translations). Lists German stage productions, with reviews. Critic index.

SHAW

E240 *Shaw: The Annual of Bernard Shaw Studies.* University Park: Pennsylvania State Univ. Press, 1981—. Annual.

(Formerly *Shaw Review*, 1957–80, and *Shaw Bulletin*, 1951–56.)

Carries a "Continuing Checklist of Shaviana," with international coverage of editions, books, articles, pamphlets, dissertations, and recordings. Now annual, this formerly appeared in each issue.

SHELLEY

(B52) *Keats-Shelley Journal.*

Lists studies on Shelley and his circle: Mary Shelley, Godwin, Peacock.

SPENSER

E243 *Spenser Newsletter.* Amherst: Univ. of Massachusetts, 1970—. 3/yr.

Each issue prints book reviews and abstracts of recent articles.

STAËL

E246 *Cahiers Staëliens.* Paris: Attinger, 1962—. Annual.

(Supersedes *Occident et Cahiers Staëliens*, 1930–39.)

Bibliographies in nearly every issue, 1930—, list international books, articles, and dissertations.

STENDHAL

E249 *Stendhal Club: Revue Trimestrielle.* Grenoble: Stendhal Club, 1958—. 4/yr.

"Bibliographie Stendhal" in each October issue is an international, comprehensive bibliography of editions (including translations), sales, studies (books, reviews, articles, and notes), and radio and television programs. Critic and subject index.

STEVENS

E252 *Wallace Stevens Journal.* Northridge, Calif.: Wallace Stevens Soc., 1977—. 4/yr.

"Current Bibliography" in each issue lists international books and articles. Carries abstracts of recent dissertations.

STORM
E255 *Theodor-Storm Gesellschaft: Schriften.* Heide: Theodor-Storm Gesellschaft, 1952—. Annual.
"Storm Bibliographie" lists editions, translations, letters, and studies
(mainly German books, articles, and dissertations).

JANE AND JESSE STUART
(E165) *Jack London Newsletter.*
"Jesse and Jane Stuart: A Bibliography Supplement" in each issue,
Vol. 2—, No. 3—, 1969—, lists works by and about Jesse Stuart and
Jane Stuart, his daughter.
This supplements Hensley C. Woodbridge, *Jesse and Jane Stuart: A
Bibliography,* 2nd ed. (Murray, Ky.: Murray State Univ., 1969).

SUARÈS
(C25) *La Revue des Lettres Modernes.*
André Suarès is a subseries, 1973—.

SWIFT
(B43) *The Scriblerian and the Kit-Cats.*
Carries abstracts of international articles on Swift and other writers of
his period.

TASSO
E258 *Studi Tassiani.* Bergamo: Secomandi, 1951—. Annual.
Carries an annual bibliographic review, for 1952— (in No. 3—,
1953—), of international books and articles on Tasso.
"Bibliografia Tassiana," an appendix to each issue, No. 3—, 1953—,
attempts to record all published commentary on Tasso.

TENNYSON
E261 *Tennyson Research Bulletin.** Lincoln: Tennyson Research Centre,
1967—. Annual.
Carries a checklist of current international books, articles, and work in
progress.

THACKERAY
E263 *The Thackeray Newsletter.* Mississippi State: Mississippi State Univ.,
1977—. 2/yr.
Lists work in progress on Thackeray (including theses and dissertations), as well as abstracts of recent and forthcoming publications and locations of manuscripts.

THOREAU
E266 *Thoreau Society Bulletin.* Geneseo, N.Y.: Thoreau Soc., 1941—. 4/yr.
"Additions to the Thoreau Bibliography," in each issue, is an interna-
tional list of current books, reviews, pamphlets, and articles.
Cumulated: *Bibliography of the Thoreau Society Bulletins 1941–
1969: A Cumulation and Index* (Troy, N.Y.: Whitston, 1971).

TOLKIEN
(E162) *Mythlore*.
Tolkien studies are listed in the quarterly "Inklings Bibliography."

UNAMUNO
E269 *Cuadernos de la Cátedra Miguel de Unamuno*. Salamanca: Universidad de Salamanca, 1948—. Annual.
"Bibliographia Unamuniana," Vol. 18—, 1968—, is an international list of books, articles, dissertations (including those in progress), editions, and upcoming conferences.

VALÉRY
(C25) *La Revue des Lettres Modernes*.
Paul Valéry is a subseries, 1974—.

VERNE
(C25) *La Revue des Lettres Modernes*.
Jules Verne is a subseries, 1975—.

WAUGH
E272 *Evelyn Waugh Newsletter*. Garden City, N.Y.: Nassau Community College, 1967—. 3/yr.
"Evelyn Waugh: A Supplementary Checklist of Criticism," Vol. 2—, 1968—, is an international list of books, articles, and dissertations.

WELTY
E275 *Eudora Welty Newsletter*. Toledo, Ohio: Univ. of Toledo, 1977—. 2/yr.
An annual "Checklist of Welty Scholarship" covers international books, articles, and dissertations.

WHITMAN
E278 *Walt Whitman Review*. Detroit: Wayne State Univ. Press, 1955—. 4/yr. (Formerly *Walt Whitman Newsletter*, 1955–58.)
Each issue carries an international list of books, reviews, articles, dissertations, and theses, as well as editions, translations, and letters and other manuscript materials.

WHITTIER
E281 *Whittier Newsletter*. Gainesville: Univ. of Florida, 1966—. 2/yr.
Carries an annual, selective review of Whittier scholarship and work in progress.

CHARLES WILLIAMS
(E162) *Mythlore*.
Williams studies are listed in "The Inklings Bibliography" in each issue.

WILLIAM CARLOS WILLIAMS
E284 *William Carlos Williams Review*. Middletown, Pa.: Capitol Campus, Pennsylvania State Univ., 1975—. 2/yr.

(Titled *William Carlos Williams Newsletter,* Vol. 1–5, 1975–79.)
Each issue lists dissertations in progress or recently completed.

WOLFE
E287   *The Thomas Wolfe Newsletter.* Akron, Ohio: Univ. of Akron, 1977—.
2/yr.
"The Wolfe Pack: Bibliography" in each issue is an international list of books and articles, with brief annotations.

WORDSWORTH
E290   *The Wordsworth Circle.* Philadelphia: Temple Univ., 1970—. 4/yr.
"Wordsworth Scholarship: An Annual Register," in the summer issue, is a bibliographic essay covering international books, articles, and dissertations. In addition, the journal carries about twenty book reviews per issue.

YEATS
(E84)   *Yeats Eliot Review.*
"Bibliographical Update" in each issue lists current international books and articles.

ZOLA
E293   *Les Cahiers Naturalistes. Bulletin.* Paris: Fasquell, 1955—. Annual.
"Bibliographie" is an international, classified list of new editions and translations and of books, articles, and dissertations on Zola.

Bibliography

The two chief sources of information about current serial bibliographies were library reference collections and card catalogs, particularly those at Columbia University and the New York Public Library, and bibliographies themselves, particularly the MLA and MHRA bibliographies and the *Bibliographic Index*. Additional sources are listed here.

Abstracting Services: Annotated Directory. 2 vols. The Hague: International Federation for Documentation, 1969.

Altick, Richard D., and Andrew Wright. *Selective Bibliography for the Study of English and American Literature.* 6th ed. New York: Macmillan, 1979.

Bassan, Fernande, Paul F. Reed, and Donald C. Spinelli. *An Annotated Bibliography of French Language and Literature.* New York: Garland, 1976.

Bell, Inglis F., and Jennifer Gallup. *A Reference Guide to English, American, and Canadian Literature: An Annotated Checklist of Bibliographical and Other Reference Materials.* Vancouver: Univ. of British Columbia Press, 1971.

Bibliography, Documentation, Terminology. Paris: UNESCO, 1961–79.

Bleznick, Donald W. "A Guide to Journals in the Hispanic Field: A Selected Annotated List of Journals Central to the Study of Spanish and Spanish American Language and Literature." *Hispania,* 49 (1966), 569–83; 52 (1969), 723–37; 55 (1972), 207–21.

——. *A Sourcebook for Hispanic Literature and Language. A Selected, Annotated Guide to Spanish and Spanish American Bibliography, Literature, Linguistics, Journals, and Other Source Materials.* Philadelphia: Temple Univ. Press, 1974.

Chicorel Index to Abstracting and Indexing Services: Periodicals in Humanities and the Social Sciences. 2 vols. New York: Chicorel, 1974.

Farley, Judith. "Author! Author! Newsletters of American Authors, A Bibliography." *Library of Congress Information Bulletin,* 36 (1977), 800–02.

Faulhaber, Uwe K., and Penrith B. Goff. *German Literature: An Annotated Reference Guide.* New York: Garland, 1979.

Fisher, John H. "Serial Bibliographies in the Modern Languages and Literatures." *PMLA,* 66 (1951), 138–53.

"From Seattle to Schenectady: More Book Reviews." *Coda: Poets & Writers Newsletter,* 6 (1978), 21–24.

Gray, Richard A. *Serial Bibliographies in the Humanities and Social Sciences.* Ann Arbor: Pierian, 1969.

Greene, Donald. "'More than a Necessary Chore': *The Eighteenth-Century Current Bibliography* in Retrospect and Prospect." *Eighteenth-Century Studies*, 10 (1976–77), 94–110.

Hartman, Charles. "Recent Publications on Chinese Literature: I. The Republic of China (Taiwan)." *Chinese Literature: Essays, Articles, Reviews*, 1 (1979), 81–86.

Harzfeld, Lois A. *Periodical Indexes in the Social Sciences and Humanities: A Subject Guide*. Metuchen, N.J.: Scarecrow, 1978.

Horecky, Paul, ed. *East Central Europe: A Guide to Basic Publications*. Chicago: Univ. of Chicago Press, 1969.

———, ed. *Southeastern Europe: A Guide to Basic Publications*. Chicago: Univ. of Chicago Press, 1969.

Irregular Serials and Annuals: An International Directory. 5th ed. New York: Bowker, 1978.

Kujoth, Jean Spealman. *Subject Guide to Periodical Indexes and Review Indexes*. Metuchen, N.J.: Scarecrow, 1969.

Lloréns, Ana M. R. "Bibliographic Indexes to Periodical Literature in the Romance Languages." *Modern Language Journal*, 60 (1976), 23–30.

McMallin, B. J. "Indexing the Periodical Literature of Anglo-American Bibliography." *Studies in Bibliography*, 33 (1980), 1–17.

Palfrey, Thomas B., Joseph G. Fucilla, William C. Holbrook. *Bibliographical Guide to the Romance Languages and Literatures*. 8th ed. Evanston: Chandler's, 1971.

Patterson, Margaret C. *Author Newsletters and Journals: An International Annotated Bibliography of Serial Publications Concerned with the Life and Works of Individual Authors*. Detroit: Gale, 1979.

———. "V.I.P. Publications: An International Bibliography of 300 Newsletters, Journals, and Miscellanea." *Bulletin of Bibliography*, 30 (1973), 156–69.

Reynolds, Michael M. *A Guide to Theses and Dissertations: An Annotated, International Bibliography of Bibliographies*. Detroit: Gale, 1975.

Rouse, Richard H., J. H. Claxton, and M. D. Metzger. *Serial Bibliographies for Medieval Studies*. Berkeley: Univ. of California Press, 1969.

Schweik, Robert C., and Dieter Riesner. *Reference Sources in English and American Literature: An Annotated Bibliography*. New York: Norton, 1977.

Sheehy, Eugene P., ed. *Guide to Reference Books*. 9th ed. Chicago: American Library Assn., 1976; supplement, 1979.

Shilstone, Marion, and Wojczech Zalewski. "Current Bibliographies in Russian and Soviet Area Studies." *Russian Review*, 37 (1978), 313–22.

Totok, Wilhelm, Karl-Heinz Weismann, and Rolf Weitzel, eds. *Handbuch der bibliographischen Nachschlagewerke*. 4th ed. Frankfurt am Main: Klostermann, 1972.

Ulrich's International Periodicals Directory. 18th ed. New York: Bowker, 1979.

Vesenyi, Paul E. *An Introduction to Periodical Bibliography*. Ann Arbor: Pierian, 1974.

Walford, A. J., ed. *Guide to Reference Material*. Vol. I, 4th ed., Vols. II and III, 3d ed. London: Library Assn., 1975–80.

Index

The best index would have been an analytical subject index that referred in detail to the coverage of all the serial bibliographies listed in this *Guide*. It was not possible to make such an index, however. Instead, I have compiled a title, author, and modified subject index to this bibliography. Included here are the titles of all the books and periodicals mentioned in Chapters i through vi and titles of many of the serial bibliographies contained in books and periodicals. These last have been included only when they are descriptive or unique. Thus, those bibliographies with titles such as "Recent Studies" are not included, nor are those that essentially repeat the title of their host periodical, such as "Restoration and Eighteenth-Century Theatre Research Bibliography" in *Restoration and Eighteenth Century Theatre Research*. In many cases I have inverted the titles of these bibliographic articles and listed them under a key word, such as "Southern Literature, A Checklist of Scholarship on." A periodical with a multiple title, such as *Romanische Bibliographie/Bibliographie Romane/Romance Bibliography*, is indexed under all versions.

Authors who are the subject of bibliographies are listed in Chapter vi and, therefore, not indexed, but the names of authors, editors, and compilers of bibliographies, if they have been mentioned in the text, are indexed.

The subjects indexed here consist of all the national literatures included in the *MLA International Bibliography* and covered in Chapters iii and iv (the specific section in the *MLAIB* is indicated if the national literature is not noted in its table of contents), the sections and subsections in Chapter v, and the subjects of individual bibliographies. These last often are indexed only under the title of the bibliography.

Numerals preceded by a capital letter refer to item numbers in this *Guide*.